Christmas
Creations

Christmas Creations

JANE BERRY

CHILTON BOOK COMPANY

RADNOR, PENNSYLVANIA

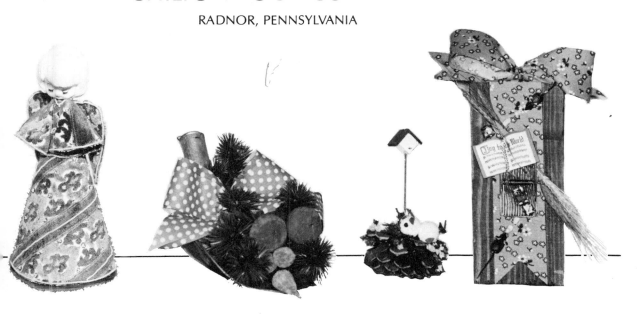

Copyright © 1974 by Jane Berry
First Edition   All Rights Reserved
Published in Radnor, Pa., by Chilton Book Company
and simultaneously in Ontario, Canada, by
Thomas Nelson & Sons, Ltd.
Designed by William E. Lickfield
Photographs by Gary Pugh, Media, Pa.
Manufactured in the United States of America

Library of Congress Cataloging in Publication Data

Berry, Jane.
  Christmas creations.
  1. Christmas decorations.   I. Title.
TT900.C4B47   745.59'41   74-12214
ISBN 0-8019-6141-6
ISBN 0-8019-6142-4 (pbk.)

To My Jack

Acknowledgments

I would like to acknowledge the able assistance of my daughter, Sue, and my husband. Also, thanks to the rest of my family, John, Jim, Janet and Julia, and to my editor, Crissie Lossing, for helping in many ways. Without them, this book would not have been written.

Many thanks to the following people for the ideas they shared with us:

Pat Daniels, Springfield, PA S-Shaped Pine Cone Centerpiece, Satin People Ornaments, and the Panoramic Ball with Music Box

Sue Berry, Media, PA Swing-A-Long Santa, Sue's Design, and Hobby and Choo-Choo Stockings

Eunice Jenkins, Olney, IL Mom's Tree Skirt and Stocking, Crocheted Snowman, and Mom's Santa

Everett Jenkins, Olney, IL Christmas Birdhouse

Mildred Jansen, Newton, IL Millie's Creation

Arlene Pugh, Media, PA Arlene's Golden Tree

Also thanks to these craft shops:

Make It Happen Craft Studio, Broomall, PA 19008 Mousetrap, Mouse-in-a-Walnut, Thread Cone Wreath, Tinsel Tree Painting, and Sandy Santa

Cottage Crafts, Malvern, PA 19355 The Wisemen

The Olive Street Craft Shop, Media, PA 19063 Matilda, Velvet Evergreen

Contents

List of Illustrations

List of Color Illustrations

Mittens for Your Door
Satin People Ornaments
Hallway Holly
Millie's Creation
Yarn Wreath
Mom's Santa
Designer Set, Wreath Place Mat
 and Napkin Ring, Jolly Santa
White Branch a'Hanging
Panoramic Ball with Music Box
Arlene's Golden Tree
More Bazaar Quickies
Matilda, Velvet Evergreen, Snow
 Fun, Della Robbia Tree

On Front Cover:
 White Fantasy
 Bazaar Quickies
 S-Shaped Pine Cone Centerpiece,
  Lacy Topiary, Bells and Bows,
  Kiddies' Treasure

On Back Cover:
 Door Knob Decorations
 Angel on a Mat, Wisemen,
  Nativity

Before You Begin

Chapter
1

PREPARATION

A place to spread out your work and leave it undisturbed for short periods of time is helpful, but not essential. A table reserved for your craft creations in the basement or in a corner of the family room is very convenient. But, the kitchen table is quite adequate if you plan your work so that glue or paint is dry when it is time to clear the table for meals. Your work area should be covered with old newspaper so as to catch bits of glue, clippings, drips, and paint overspray for easy clean up.

A storage area to keep your supplies separate, but handy, can be a shelf in the linen closet or near your work table. Shoe boxes work very well for keeping supplies and tools neatly stored away. You may identify the contents of each box by writing on the end with a felt tip pen.

Tools and household items that can be readily used in completing projects are:

Decoupage scissors	Scissors
Gloves	Serrated knife
Masking tape	Soft rags
Needle with large eye	Straight pins
Needle nose pliers	Tissue paper
Paper towels	Toothpicks
Pencil and notebook	Various sizes nylon bristle
Pinking shears	paint brushes
Posterboard	Wax paper
Ruler	Wire cutters

Materials that are used quite often on many different projects are:

Craft sticks	Silicone sealer
Fern pins	Spool #28 wire
Floral adhesive	White glue

Leftover items of craft materials, beads, ribbon, braid, decorations, and sequins are best saved for your next project, or the idea you may have tomorrow.

MATERIALS AND SUPPLIES

The materials described in this book are available at most retail craft stores. The remainder may be purchased at a fabric store or a hardware store. Extra material, scraps, or parts of packaged items may be saved for other projects. Be sure to close caps, lids, or package fasteners tightly to preserve the contents.

White glue is a universal adhesive, fastener, or sealer. It is applied easily, holds tightly, and dries clear. While the glue is wet, it may be easily wiped off with a damp cloth. After drying, it is almost impossible to remove. So be neat while applying the glue, and clean up the drips and smears promptly. Gr. r. rip ® is strongly recommended.

Felt material is easy to cut and use. It may be stretched and shaped to fit rounded surfaces without tearing.

To keep the streamer ends of ribbons and bows from raveling, apply a thin line of white glue across the back of the ribbon where it is to be cut. After the glue is dry, cut the ribbon splitting the line of glue.

Chenille comes in several sizes and shapes. The chenille bumps and stems used for projects described in this book have a wire center. Thus, they are easily shaped and fastened to Styrofoam® or other materials. Chenille is available from D. Jay Products, Inc., P.O. Box 797, Newark, NJ 07107.

The following directions cover items which are called for in several projects. It would be well to practice these and develop your technique before starting a project.

MAKE A BOW

4

These are general instructions for making a bow. The width of the ribbon depends on the project. Once you have mastered this technique, you will want to put a bow on everything you make.

Materials

2 yd, 4" (76") of ribbon   12" of #28 wire

Cut 4 inches from the length of ribbon and set aside. With the long length, make an 8-inch loop, leaving loose about 12 inches for a streamer (Fig. 1-1). Make another 8-inch loop on the other side and lead the ribbon to the back. Catch the ribbon at the center after each loop. Repeat the above steps to make six loops (Fig. 1-2).

Fold the length of wire over the center of the bow (Fig. 1-3). Twist the wire near the ribbon, leaving the ends free in order to attach the bow to your projects. Cut the 4 inches of ribbon in half lengthwise and glue it over the wire to hide it.

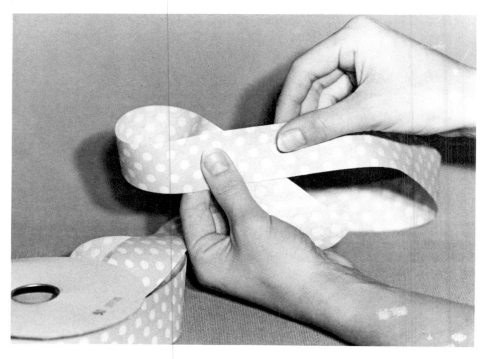

Fig. 1-1 Forming first loop for bow.

Fig. 1-2 Catching loop at center.

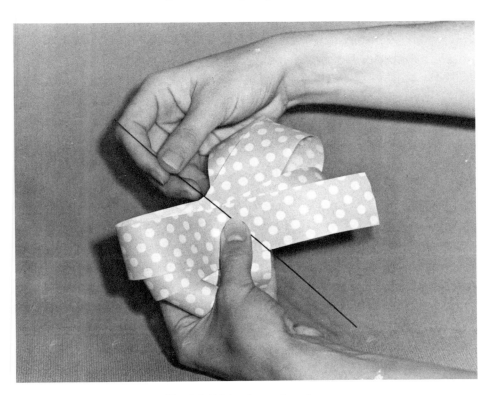

Fig. 1-3 Wiring bow at center.

MAKE A CIRCLE

Remember that a 12-inch *diameter* circle has a *radius* of 6 inches. Also, some of the patterns for cones have dimensions for the radius.

If you do not have a compass to inscribe a circle, the following technique works very well.

Using string and a pencil, tie the string in a slip knot around the pencil and pull tight. Lay the material to be marked on a flat surface, with a ruler laying nearby. Holding the pencil vertically and at the zero end of the ruler, measure the length of string to equal the *radius* of the circle required. Pinch the string, at the required distance, with your other hand. Your thumbnail is a good marker for the center point.

Hold the pencil and string firmly. Place your thumbnail, which marks the center, in the middle of the material to be cut. With the pencil held in a vertical position, swing the pencil point in an arc, thus marking the circle required (Fig. 1-4).

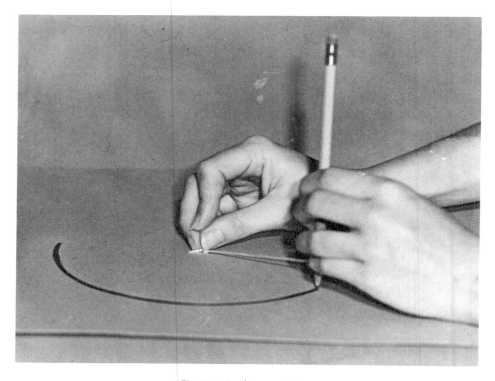

Fig. 1-4 Scribing a circle.

MAKE A CORNER

Trimming plaques or hangings with wide, flat ribbon quite often requires that a corner be turned. A neater project can be accomplished if the ribbon is turned, instead of cutting the ribbon and starting again.

7

Spread glue on the surface where the ribbon is to be fastened. Press the ribbon into the glue, smoothing the ribbon as you proceed to the corner. At the corner, fold the ribbon back in the direction from where it has been glued. Apply glue along the ribbon at the fold, equal to the width of the ribbon. Now fold the ribbon again, diagonally across itself and in the direction of the new line or edge to be followed. Continue fastening with glue. At the folded corner, work glue under the folded edge, using a toothpick.

Centerpieces

Chapter
2

Holly Wood

Materials

Natural tree bark	Christmas greens
Small Christmas song book	Candle

While our sons were cutting firewood, I noticed this interesting piece of bark that had split off a log. The bark had possibilities so I placed it end down to form the base of a table decoration (Fig. 2-1).

Fig. 2-1 Materials for Holly Wood.

10

Random lengths of Christmas greens are placed inside the bark. Now set a small Christmas song book at the top edge of the bark with the candle set at either side.

It takes only a few minutes to create this centerpiece (Fig. 2-9) that will complement your dinner table or buffet.

Arlene's Golden Tree

(SEE COLOR INSERT)

Materials

25 yd gold nylon net material, 72" wide

3 yd 1½" green velvet ribbon

5½ yd of 1½" gold velvet ribbon

60 green Christmas tree balls, 1" diam.

27 gold plastic bells, 1½" diam.

7 medium size white pine cones, closed

7 medium size white pine cones, open

20" x 20" of ¼" plywood

30" x 40" of ½" hardware cloth

6 spools #28 wire

Two 3" plastic angels

String of 50 miniature Christmas tree lights

Gold glitter

Gold spray paint

Spray glue

¼" wire staples

Wire cutters, pliers, and gloves

String

Felt tip pen

Lay the wire hardware cloth on a flat surface. Using a 26-inch long string for the radius and a felt tip pen for the marker, mark off one-third of a circle on the wire cloth. One-third of a circle is that part of a clock from 12 o'clock to 4 o'clock (Fig. 2-2). Using wire cutters, cut out the one-third circle. Be sure to wear heavy cloth or leather gloves while cutting the wire hardware cloth to protect your hands. Now cut off one inch of wire cloth at the point of the one-third circle.

Roll and shape the wire hardware cloth into a cone. Overlap the edges 1½ inches and secure tightly by twisting short lengths of #28 wire through the wire cloth at five or six places along the overlapped material. Form and shape the wire cloth until the surface is smooth and even.

Cut the plywood into a 3-inch wide ring, having an outside diameter of 17 inches and an inside diameter of 11 inches (Fig. 2-3). Now set the wire cloth cone onto the plywood ring; be sure the cone is centered on the ring and fastened with wire staples.

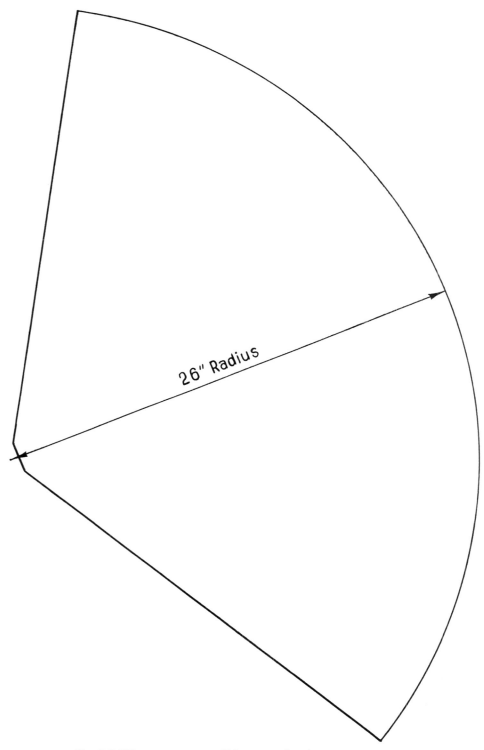

26" Radius

Fig. 2-2 Wire cone pattern. This pattern has been reduced: ¾″ = 4″

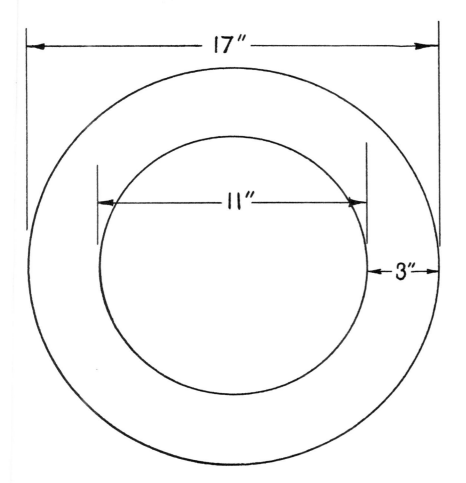

Fig. 2-3 Wood base pattern. This pattern has been reduced: 1″ = 4″

Spray paint the wire cone and wood ring gold. Be sure to spread plenty of old newspapers over the work surface. Spread the pine cones over the newspaper and spray paint them gold also. While the paint is still tacky, sprinkle gold glitter lightly over the pine cones. Allow the paint to dry.

Cut the entire piece of nylon net into 5 by 36-inch strips. Cut 8-inch lengths of #28 wire. Fold and gather each strip of nylon net tightly. Gathered material is to be five inches wide. Wrap a single piece of wire around the center of the gathered material, pull and twist the wire tightly. Spread the edges of the gathered material and fluff up into a poof. Continue gathering, wiring, and fluffing until all the cut material is made into poofs.

13

Place the poofs onto the wire cone by starting at the top. Wire the poof onto the wire hardware cloth by putting each of the tie wires through a different opening and then twisting the wires tightly from inside the cone. Continue wiring the poofs to the cone, spacing them 2 to 2½ inches apart, until the wire cone is completely covered.

Start decorating and trimming the tree by placing the string of miniature lights on first. Insert each light through the hardware cloth and net poofs from inside the tree. Space the individual lights evenly over the tree. The lights should be placed so that their ends are even with the ends of the net poofs.

Cut the green velvet ribbon in half and form two 6-inch single loop bows. Wrap an 8-inch length of wire around the centers and twist tightly. Set one of the bows about two-thirds the way up the tree, push the tie wire through the net and from inside the tree twist the ends around the wire hardware cloth to fasten. Drape the ribbon streamers down and around the tree. Catch each streamer in three evenly spaced places with an 8-inch length of wire. Push the wire through the net, and twist ends around wire cloth to secure the ribbon streamers. Place second green bow on opposite side of the tree, repeat the above steps to arrange and fasten the bow and streamers.

Next, cut the gold velvet ribbon into 14-inch lengths. Make a single loop bow with each length of ribbon. Tie securely at center by wrapping an 8-inch length of wire around the bow and twisting tightly. Spray each bow lightly with glue, and sprinkle a small amount of gold glitter on each bow. Allow the glue to dry. Arrange the gold bows evenly on the tree. Fasten by pushing the tie wires through the net and from inside the tree, twist the tie wire around the wire cloth.

Fasten the green Christmas tree balls into groups of three, passing an 8-inch length of wire through the loop on each ball and twisting the wire. Arrange the clusters of balls evenly on the tree. Fasten to the tree by pushing the tie wire through the net and from inside the tree twist the tie wire around the wire cloth.

Twist an 8-inch length of wire around the stem end of each pine cone. Arrange the pine cones evenly on the tree and fasten in the same manner as for the Christmas tree balls.

Gather the plastic bells into groups of three. Hold the bells together with an 8-inch length of wire and twist the wire. Arrange the cluster of bells evenly on the tree and fasten in the same manner as for the Christmas tree balls.

The angels are the last items to be put on the tree. Twist an 8-inch length of wire around the base of each angel. Set the angels on top of the tree and push the tie wires through the net. From inside the tree, twist the tie wires around the wire cloth.

Lacy Topiary
(SEE FRONT COVER)

For this project, we use a lacy ribbon that has a gathering thread running through the top. You just pull the thread and immediately you have a nice poof.

Materials

5″ Styrofoam ball	10 white chenille stems
3″ Styrofoam ball	6 red chenille stems
18 yd of 3″ red lace ribbon, or Lacelon®	3 yd silver braid
	18″ dowel
28 yd of 3″ white lace ribbon, or Lacelon	Sticky floral clay
	Red paint
18 silver balls, 1″ diam., with stems	Vase

Cut eighteen one-yard pieces of red lace. Also, cut twenty-eight one-yard lengths of white lace. Pull the gathering thread tight on all pieces of lace and tie the ends together.

Cut all chenille stems into 4-inch lengths and form them into U shapes. Push a red chenille stem through the ends of the center of each red poof and push the ends of a white chenille stem through the center of each white poof.

Push four red poofs into the Styrofoam ball in one area. Directly opposite these poofs, push four more red poofs into the Styrofoam.

Make one row of white poofs around both clusters of red poofs. For the center row, alternate red and white poofs to completely cover the ball. Push the stem of the silver balls in the center of the single red poofs and one silver ball in the center of one of the red clusters. This will be the top.

Paint the dowel red. Let dry. Using the sticky clay, secure the small Styrofoam ball in vase. When the dowel has dried, push it in the center of the Styrofoam in the vase. Then, insert the dowel into the bottom center of the red cluster. Make sure it is centered.

Make a bow with the silver braid and use a chenille stem to attach it to the ball next to the dowel. To cover the Styrofoam in the vase, put three poofs around the dowel. As easy as that, you have a charming topiary.

Della Robbia Tree

(SEE COLOR INSERT)

This tree is really fun and inexpensive to make. In addition to being an attractive centerpiece, it is also a lovely holiday gift for a neighbor, teacher, friend, or relative. Try it.

Materials

12″ Styrofoam cone	2 dozen small plastic fruits
Bag unshelled mixed nuts	Acoustical tile gum glue
Pine cones, various sizes	Old case knife

Spread the unshelled nuts on a cookie sheet and bake in a 200°F oven for one hour to keep them from spoiling. While the unshelled nuts are cooling, sort the pine cones by size. Pine cones which are over 1½ inches in diameter should be cut into halves or thirds. Also, cover your work surface with newspaper and place an 18-inch piece of wax paper on the newspaper. Set the Styrofoam cone on the wax paper. The cone may be turned while you are working by turning the wax paper.

Using an old case knife, spread gum glue over a 4-inch square area of the cone, starting at the bottom of the cone. Selecting from the larger sizes, press pine cones hard into the gum glue. Avoid getting gum glue on your hands. Vary the pattern of the pine cones by placing some right side up, others bottom side up, and still others sideways. Alternate the placement of every other pine cone. Place a pecan, brazil nut, or large acorn every so often in the arrangement of pine cones. When the gum glue area is covered, proceed around the bottom of the Styrofoam cone with gum glue and placement of pine cones and nuts.

After completing one row around the bottom of the Styrofoam cone, the next row up should use medium size pine cones and mixed nuts. The top area of the Styrofoam cone should be covered with smallest pine cones or pieces of pine cones and the smallest of the mixed nuts. Cover all gum glued areas with pine cones or mixed nuts.

As a finishing touch, fill in some of the spaces with small plastic fruit. These are fastened by pushing their wire stems into the Styrofoam cone. The tree can also be trimmed by adding bows or bits of old jewelry.

Fig. 2-4 Angels, large and small.

Angels

This is a delightful figure for a table centerpiece, fireplace mantle, or Christmas scene (Fig. 2-4). You can use felt or leftover fabric from drapes or upholstery material.

Materials

12" x 36" felt or fabric	Masking tape
12" x 18" poster board	Straight pins
Doll head	White glue
Braid or pearls	

Using the pattern outlines in Figs. 2-5 and 2-6, cut out the following items:

Felt skirt	Poster board wing
Poster board skirt	Felt cape and arms
2 felt wings	

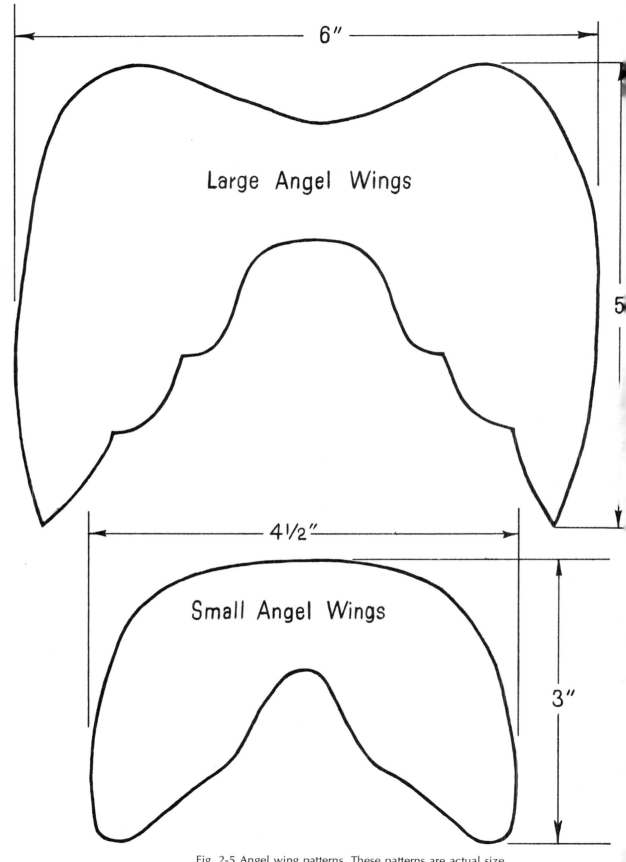

6"

Large Angle Wings

5

4½"

Small Angle Wings

3"

Fig. 2-5 Angel wing patterns. These patterns are actual size.

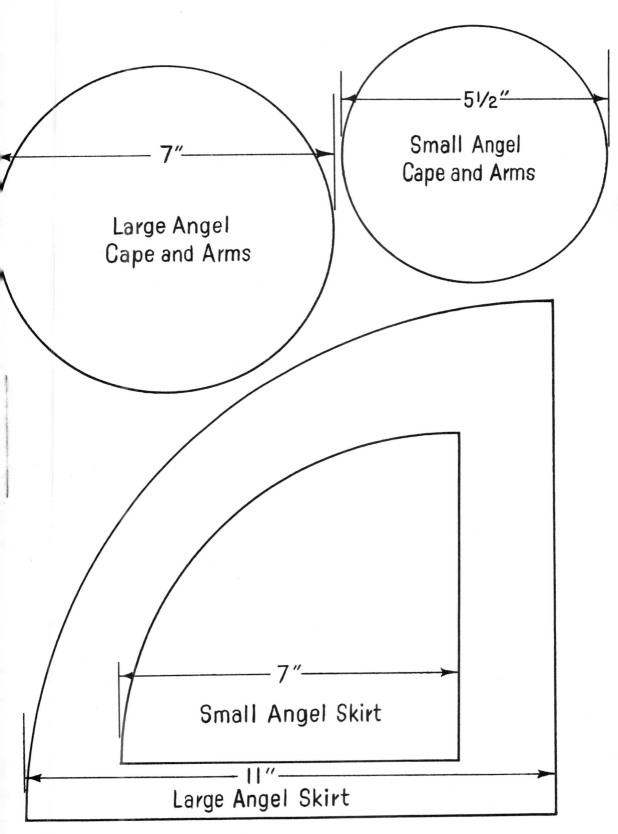

Fig. 2-6 Angel skirt and cape patterns. These patterns have been reduced: 1″ = 2″

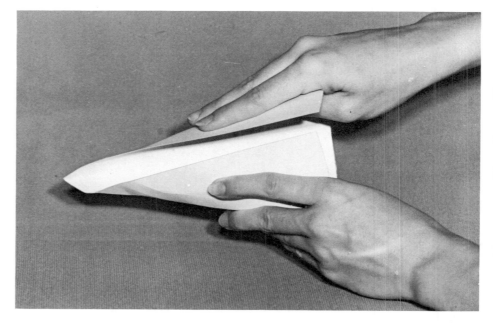

Fig. 2-7 Forming the cone base.

Roll the poster board skirt into a smooth cone shape (Fig. 2-7). Overlap the seam ½ inch and secure with masking tape on both sides. Cut ½ inch off the top of the cone.

Lay skirt material, reverse side up, on work table. Apply white glue on all outside edges of the cone. Roll the poster board cone over the skirt material, thus covering the cone. Secure the seam in the material with glue. Glue braid or pearls at the skirt bottom. Using glue, trim remainder of skirt with braid or pearls in your own design.

Glue one piece of wing material to each side of the poster board wing. Trim the wing edges with braid or pearls.

Fold the cape material into quarters. Cut a small hole at the point of the folded material. Lay cape flat on table and trim edge with braid or pearls.

Assemble the angel by placing the cape with the hole over the top of the cone. Bring cape together at each side of the cone, forming the arms. Apply glue on the inside of the fabric to hold the arms. Pull upper side of arms toward front of angel. Pin bottom edge of arms to cone to hold arms in a natural position.

Insert the stick that the doll head is mounted on through the hole in the cape and glue the head in position desired. Glue wings onto the back of the cone and your angel is ready for display.

Wisemen

(SEE BACK COVER)

Materials

Three 12" Styrofoam cones
3 antiqued plastic kings' heads
3 pairs antiqued plastic men's
    hands
Six 12" x 12" felt, one
    square of each color:
    turquoise, lime green,
    magenta, hot pink, rust,
    and gold
1⅔ yd gold, red, and green
    round braid
1⅔ yd of ¼" gold
    double loop braid
1⅔ yd of ½" gold flat braid

15" of ¾" gold loop braid
    with sequins
21" of ½" brown gimp
15" of 1" gold flat braid
4½ yd of #16 wire
Package of 3 plaster of
    paris objects to
    represent gifts
Assorted braid and sequins
Masking tape
Tissue paper
White glue
Pliers

Sort the heads, hands, felt, braid, and gifts into three sets of matching items for creating a wiseman out of each Styrofoam cone. The directions are for one wiseman, but all three can be created concurrently.

Cut three skirts from three pieces of felt (magenta, rust, turquoise) following the pattern outline in Fig. 2-8. Starting 3 inches down from the top of the Styrofoam cone, glue the skirts to the cones. Be sure to match the curves of the felt to the bottom edges of the cones. Overlap the seams ⅛ inch and hold the felt with pins while the glue dries.

Cut the wire into three equal pieces. Measure one inch down from the top of the cone. At this point, gently push one piece of wire horizontally through the cone. Equal lengths of wire should extend from each side of the cone. Bend each end of the wire to form a small hook. Wrap some tissue paper around each hook and glue in place. Force the hooks and paper into the plastic hands; hold the hands in place with masking tape. Crumple tissue paper and drape over wire next to the cone to form shoulders and upper arms. Use masking tape to hold paper in place. Bend wire to form elbows. Now bend and form wire so that hands are positioned together in front of the figure.

Glue the smaller gold braid trim around the four sides of the

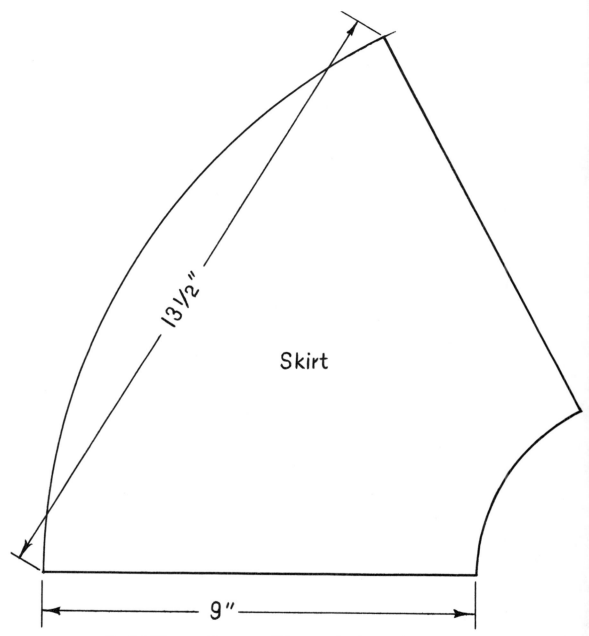

Fig. 2-8 Wisemen skirt pattern. This pattern has been reduced: 1″ = 2″

second piece of felt. Cut a small circle in the center of the felt. Slip the top of a cone through the hole in the felt. Glue the edge of the felt hole onto the cone ½ inch from the top.

Drape the felt cape over and under the arms. Smooth the cape to fit the cone body. Glue cape together under the arms; pin until dry. Glue the felt edges together at the hands to form sleeves; pin until dry. Glue small braid trim onto the cape front and collar. Glue the head in place over the top of the cone. Be sure neck reaches the collar of the cape.

Decorate the gift with scraps of braid and sequins. Set the gift in the wiseman's hands and glue in place.

Your wisemen are now ready to offer gifts to the Christmas spirit.

Blue and Green Chenille Trees

Bump chenille decorations are fun to make. This set of trees is nice on a mantle or on a door (Fig. 2-9). Do your own thing and try it in your favorite colors.

Materials

6" Styrofoam half tree	9 yd of 3" blue bump chenille
9" Styrofoam half tree	9 yd of 3" green bump chenille
12" Styrofoam half tree	White glue

With an old pair of scissors or wire cutters, cut all the bump chenille into single bump pieces. Hold tightly one cut end between thumb and index finger. Twist chenille bump around index finger. Shape all chenille bumps in this manner.

Cover the 6-inch cone first. Dip the end of one shaped blue chenille bump into white glue and push it into the Styrofoam tree at the bottom (Fig. 2-10). You should use six blue bumps in the bottom row. In the same manner, use green chenille bumps for the second row. You should use five bumps this time. Continue to cover the cone, alternating the color for each row and decreasing the number of bumps in each row.

For the 9-inch cone, use nine chenille bumps on the bottom row and twelve rows to cover the cone in the same manner. For the 12-inch cone, cover the cone with eleven bumps on the bottom row and make fourteen rows.

If you like, trim the chenille trees with gold braid, small bows, or tiny angels.

Fig. 2-9 Chenille Trees, Holly Wood, Joy.

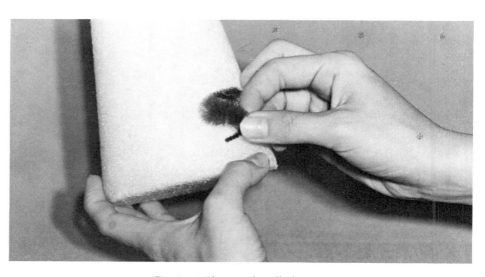

Fig. 2-10 Placing chenille bump.

S-Shaped Pine Cone Centerpiece
(SEE FRONT COVER)

Materials

12 to 18 pine cones, white tipped and Norway pine	½" paint brush
	Gold paint
18 sweet gum balls	Clear acrylic spray paint
12 red artificial apples	#24 wire
10" x 16" brown felt	Garden pruners
10" x 16" corrugated cardboard	Christmas greens
10" x 10" of ¼" hardware cloth	Wire cutters
1" wide masking tape	Gloves

Cut an 8-inch diameter circle of hardware cloth with a 4-inch center opening, using wire cutters. Wear gloves when working. Cut the circle exactly in half, and you will have two C shapes. Lay the C's on the table, facing in opposite directions to form an S.

Secure the hardware with pieces of wire where the ends meet in the center. Wrap one-inch masking tape over the edges of the S to protect hands and clothes. Trace the S shape on the cardboard, and cut out. Trace cardboard shape onto the brown felt, and cut out. Set cardboard and felt shape aside.

Select cones that are sturdy, fresh, and not dry or dark in color. The white tipped cones are used as the base cones. To make the centerpiece, approximately twelve to eighteen cones are needed. The diameter of the cone will determine the number you will actually use. I chose the tips of the cones 3 inches in length as the outer edges of the S and the bottom of the cones 2 inches in length for the inside of the S. So from a cone 5 inches in total length, you can get two pieces: one 3 inches and one 2 inches. If you have whole cones 3 inches and 2 inches in length, you will not have to cut them.

Use garden pruners to cut cones. Work the blade into and in between the petals of the cone and clip the stem. Lay out your cones on the hardware S to determine approximately how many cones you will need. Select a few more to have on hand because once the cones are wired together they become tight and a few more will fit on the form.

Each cone has to be wired individually. Place the middle cone over the center of a 9-inch piece of wire. Bring the two ends of the wire up and across the wires next to the cone. Then holding the two wires in one hand, twist the cone in the other hand. Twist the cone at least three or four times. If the wires are not exactly the same length, twist the longer wire around the shorter one to make one wire extending from the cone. Wire each cone this way. Pull the wires out from the side of the cone.

Lay two 3-inch cones side by side, very close to each other, with the tips pointing to the outer edge, on the edge of the S. Extend the cones about 2 inches over the edge. Place wire of the first cone through a hole in the hardware cloth. Then place the second cone wire in a hole close to the first one and twist the wires together on the back of the hardware cloth shape. Place the third and fourth cones next to the wired cones, being sure the wires go through separate holes. Cover both tips of the S and the outside edges with the 3-inch cones; the 3-inch cones will show the most so be sure they are in an attractive arrangement. Wire all cones on the S in the same manner.

When placing the cones on the inside of the S, keep in mind the size of the candles you will be using. Do not extend the cones too far from the edge, but just enough to cover the hardware edge. The main purpose of the base cones is to cover the outer and inner edges of the S shape; so if there are spaces on the top of the S, do not worry.

Fill the top in with wired gum balls in groups of three or four and with Norway pines. Push wires from the filler cones to the back of the S. After all the pine cones and gum balls and other decorative nuts and pods are on the S, spray the entire S top, bottom, and sides with clear acrylic. When dry, brush gold paint on the tips of the cones and then the gum balls for accent and highlights.

Group apples into four groups of three. Hold apple stems together; then twist one stem around the other two stems, being careful not to pull stems too hard. Should apples come off the stems, glue together with white glue, and let dry. If the stems are too short to go through the thickness of the base cones, use a 9-inch wire wrapped around the apple stems for an extension. Place groups of apples on each tip and on the curves. Wire greens between the apples, grouping in a pleasing manner.

Carefully turn the S over to the back and twist together as much as possible the wires that are sticking out. Carefully cut off the twisted wires with cutters; wires should be no shorter than 2 inches in length. Then push these wires against the hardware shape so none are sticking out.

Make holes in the cardboard along the edges at 4-inch intervals with the point of your scissors or with an ice pick. Wire the cardboard to the back of the hardware cloth shape with 9-inch pieces of wire. Cut the wires short after they have been twisted; then push the ends into the cones or into the cardboard. Glue the felt shape over the cardboard shape.

Place candles in the curves of the S and stand back and just wait for the compliments.

White Fantasy

(SEE FRONT COVER)

Materials

12" Styrofoam cone	2 yd of 1½" ribbon
2 dozen white plastic holly	2 candles
picks with red berries	3 white chenille stems
Two 5" Styrofoam rings	

Cut mounting wire on plastic picks to 1½ inch. Starting at the bottom of the cone, insert the pick mounting wires into the Styrofoam. Space the white plastic holly picks evenly around the cone. Continue placing the picks up and around the cone to form the tree (Fig. 2-11).

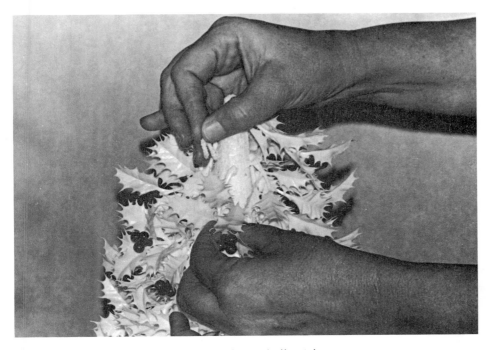

Fig. 2-11 Placing holly picks.

To form the candle rings, cover the ring tops only with plastic picks in the same manner as the cone was covered.

Cut 40 inches of ribbon for the tree. Form a double loop bow and tie at the center with white chenille stem. Attach the bow at the tree top by pushing the chenille stem into the Styrofoam. Arrange the bow streamers along the sides of the tree.

Cut the remaining ribbon in half and form a single loop bow for each of the candle rings. Tie and attach the bow to the ring with a white chenille stem. Place the candles in their rings.

Arrange the tree and candles on your dining or buffet table and you are ready for holiday visitors.

Swing-A-Long Santa

Materials

2 wire coat hangers	6" Styrofoam disk
2 yd red velvet tubing	24" of ¾" green ribbon
8" x 14" white felt	18" of ½" green ribbon
1" x 8" black felt	Two 2" Styrofoam balls
1" x 2" red felt	Two 10mm wiggle eyes
42 red chenille bumps	White glue
8 white chenille bumps	Craft stick
20 green chenille bumps	

The finished Swing-A-Long Santa is pictured in Fig. 2-12.

Cut wire coat hangers and form into two 10-inch rings, do not join ends. Pull cord from center of velvet tubing and slip tubing over the wire. Glue at each end to hold tubing on the wire.

Cut two white felt circles to fit the Styrofoam disk. Glue one piece of felt to each side of the disk. Cut a ¾-inch green ribbon to fit along the side edge of disk and fasten with glue.

To assemble the loops and disk, first center one loop on the disk and push the ends into the Styrofoam. Place the second loop at right angles to the first loop and push the ends into the Styrofoam. Apply glue around the area where the disk and loops meet. Wire the loops together at the top center.

For Santa, first cut 30 single red chenille bumps, 7 single white chenille bumps, and 4 double red chenille bumps. Take 13 single red chenille bumps and cover one Styrofoam ball. Stick one end of a red

Fig. 2-12 Mr. Snowman, Swing-A-Long Santa, Fringe Tree.

chenille bump into the ball, and stick the other end into the Styrofoam. Continue placing chenille bumps side by side around the ball until it is covered.

Now, take 10 single red chenille bumps and 3 white chenille bumps to cover the second Styrofoam ball. Start by placing the red chenille bumps side by side and finish with the white bumps. The white chenille forms Santa's face.

Use 4 white chenille bumps to make Santa's beard. Stick the end of each white bump in position, on each side of the white face bumps, bring the other ends together at the bottom and twist to hold.

For the hat, space 4 red chenille bumps evenly around the top of the head by sticking one end into the Styrofoam and bringing the other ends together at the top and twisting to hold. Place 3 red chenille bumps around the head for hat brim. Fasten by pushing ends into the Styrofoam.

To fasten Santa's head onto body, insert one half of a craft stick into the bottom of the head and then push stick into other ball to complete assembly.

Take the 4 double red chenille bumps and fold in half for use as arms and legs. Position correctly and push the chenille bump ends into the Styrofoam.

Glue wiggle eyes on face. Cut mouth from the red felt and glue in position. Cut belt from the black felt and glue into position also.

Use the remaining piece of ribbon for the swing. Glue ends over top of two rings. Set Santa in swing and bend his arms around the ribbon to hold in place.

The flowers are made from five single green chenille bumps and one single red chenille bump. Lay one end of each green bump together and twist. Spread and shape the bumps into petals. Roll the red chenille bump into a circle and glue in the center to complete the flower. Glue one flower on top of the rings and glue three flowers on the white felt base.

Now we're ready to Swing-A-Long!

Mushroom Tree

Materials

12" Styrofoam cone	½ yd of ⅜" red velvet ribbon
6 dozen large velvet rose leaves	Green spray paint
	Spray can top, for base
8 dozen small velvet rose leaves	Red paint
	White glue
3 dozen mushrooms	

The finished Mushroom Tree is pictured in Fig. 4-1.

Spray the Styrofoam cone with green paint. Let dry. Cut excess wire from the leaves and mushrooms, leaving about one inch for mounting onto the cone.

Using the large velvet leaves and starting at the bottom of the cone, arrange the leaves in rows around the cone. Fasten the leaves to the cone by pointing the wire end of the leaf toward the top of the cone, and pushing the wire into the Styrofoam. Place row after row up the cone, covering all the Styrofoam and using all the large leaves. Then start with the small leaves and complete the covering of the cone.

Arrange the mushrooms over the cone and fasten by pushing the wire into the Styrofoam. Make a bow of red velvet ribbon and fasten to the top of the cone with glue.

The base is made from a spray can top that has been painted red. Fasten the cone to the base with glue. Set the mushroom tree on a red felt circle in the center of the table.

Snow Fun

(SEE COLOR INSERT)

The wooden plaque I used in this centerpiece was cut out of a board from the old barn on the Berry homeplace in Southern Illinois.

Materials

8″ x 12″ wooden plaque	Twenty ¾″ Styrofoam balls
6″ x 6″ red felt	2 dozen cotton balls
8″ x 8″ black felt	Diamond dust
8″ red ribbon	White glue
½″ nylon brush	Small Styrofoam block
12″ black cord	Green glitter
3 red 6mm beads	Toothpicks
2 blue 6mm beads	10 straight pins
3″ Styrofoam ball	2 craft sticks
2″ Styrofoam ball	Poster board

Glue cotton balls to cover most of the board you will be using. This will be your snowy playground.

To build your snowman, insert one half of a craft stick into each of the 2-inch and 3-inch Styrofoam balls. Also, insert a toothpick into two of ¾″ Styrofoam balls. While holding the craft sticks, brush white glue to cover all four Styrofoam balls. While the glue is still wet, sprinkle diamond dust to cover the balls. To dry, insert the sticks or toothpicks into a Styrofoam block and set aside.

When the diamond dust balls are dry, remove the stick from the 3-inch ball. Break off one-half of the stick protruding from the 2-inch ball. Put glue on the remainder of the stick in the 2-inch ball, and insert into the 3-inch ball, thus joining the snowman's head and body. Put the two small balls on the body for arms by inserting the toothpicks into the 3-inch ball.

The hat is cut from black felt. Cut two 3-inch circles; one rectangle, 1½ inch by 5 inches; and one 1½-inch circle. Also, cut one poster board circle, 2¾ inches in diameter. Glue a 3-inch felt circle to each side of the poster board circle. Roll the rectangle lengthwise into a tube of 1½-inch diameter and glue the seam. Fasten the 1½-inch felt circle to one end of the felt tube with glue. Now glue the tube in the center of the 3-inch felt circle. Presto, a black hat for a snowman. Glue and pin the hat onto the snowman's head.

Cut two black felt feet and glue in place. To make the snowman's face, cut two eyebrows from the leftover black felt and cut the mouth from red felt, and glue onto the head. Using straight pins, fasten red beads to the body for buttons, and blue beads for eyes. Tie the ribbon around his neck for a scarf. Your snowman is complete.

Fifteen small Styrofoam balls will be used to make the tree. The base is six balls arranged in a triangle, joined together with toothpicks and then glued. The next two layers are three balls each, glued together in a triangle. Glue two more balls together and fasten them vertically for the tree top. Now brush white glue here and there over the tree and sprinkle with green glitter. Set aside to dry. To finish the tree, glue one small ball under the bottom layer to form the tree trunk.

Cut a sled from red felt following the pattern outline in Fig. 2-13. Cut two red felt pieces and one piece of poster board for the seat. Cut four red felt pieces and two pieces of poster board for the runners. Now glue one piece of felt to each side of matching poster board. Set aside to dry. Punch a small hole in the front end of each runner. Lay the sled seat on wax paper. Put glue on top edge of each runner and then position them on the sled seat. Let dry. Pull black cord through holes in runner and tie loose ends together.

Position the snowman, sled, and tree on the cotton covered plaque; and glue them to the board. Now your centerpiece is ready for a party.

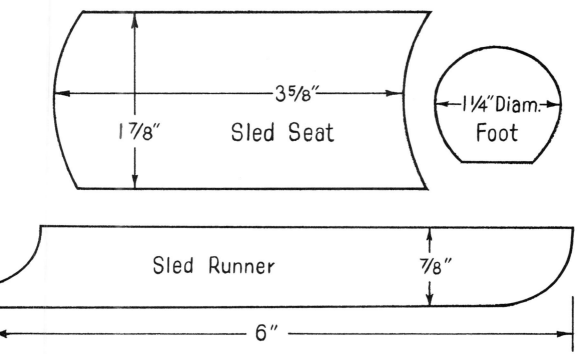

Fig. 2-13 Snow Fun patterns. These patterns are actual size.

Mr. Snowman

This snowman is great as a centerpiece, or sitting on the desk in the hall (Fig. 2-12). The children who come to visit will soon notice his hat full of goodies. Our snowman makes a fine gift for a school party.

Materials

12" Styrofoam ball	Two 25mm wiggle eyes
8" Styrofoam ball	18" x 18" black felt
150 plastic sandwich bags	18" of ½" green ribbon
26" braid trim	1 yd of 2" plaid ribbon
1 plastic strawberry	Craft stick
3 plastic blackberries	White glue
40 white chenille stems	Poster board

Flatten the 12-inch Styrofoam ball by cutting off a small slice with a serrated edge knife. Keeping the flattened side on the table, insert the craft stick into the center top of this ball. Put glue on the exposed end of the stick, and press the 8-inch ball onto it so that it sets directly atop the larger ball.

34

Fig. 2-14 Gathering plastic loop.

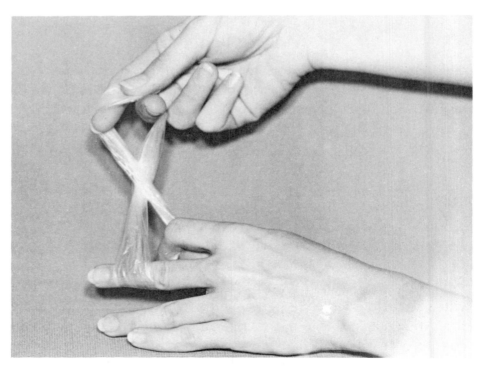

Fig. 2-15 Forming first figure eight.

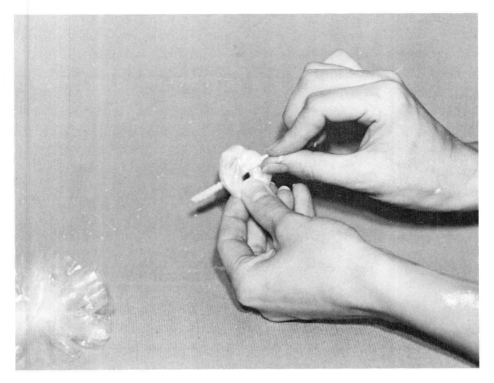

Fig. 2-16 Chenille stem through doubled loop.

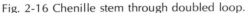

To make the plastic puffs, first cut the chenille stems into 3-inch lengths. Now cut the sealed end off all the plastic sandwich bags.

Slip one hand through the bag and gather into a plastic loop (Fig. 2-14). Twist the loop into a figure eight and fold in half to form a double loop (Figs. 2-15 and 2-16). Twist the loop again into a figure eight and form another double loop. Put a chenille stem piece through the loop and twist tightly around the plastic. Cut the loop opposite to the stem. Spread and fluff the plastic to complete the puff. Continue until all sandwich bags are formed into puffs.

Now cover the Styrofoam balls, except the flat bottom, with the puffs by pushing the chenille stem into the Styrofoam.

Using the patterns in Fig. 2-17, cut two eyes and two feet from the black felt. Also, cut two 8-inch circles and two 4-inch by 12-inch rectangles from the black felt. Cut one 8-inch circle and one 4-inch by 12-inch rectangle from the poster board.

To construct the hat, glue a black felt circle to each side of the poster board circle. Glue a black felt rectangle to each side of the poster board rectangle. Form the black felt rectangle into a 4-inch

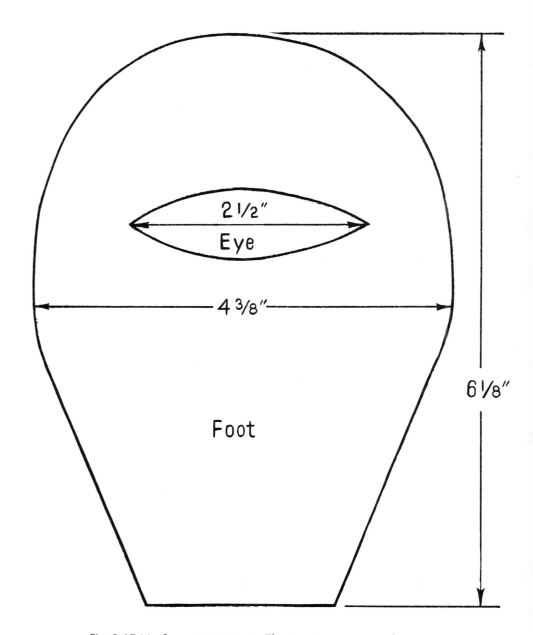

2 1/2"

Eye

4 3/8"

6 1/8"

Foot

Fig. 2-17 Mr. Snowman patterns. These patterns are actual size.

high tube, overlapping the end in ¼-inch seam, and fasten it with glue. Center the tube on the felt circle and glue it in place. Tie a bow of green ribbon and glue it to the hat. Glue the hat onto the snowman's head, tilting it to the one side if you like. Attach wiggle eyes to the black felt eye shapes with glue. Now glue the eyes onto the head.

Using the wire stems on the plastic fruit as fasteners, insert the wire on the strawberry into the Styrofoam in position for a nose. Position the three blackberries for buttons and fasten by inserting the wire stem into the Styrofoam.

Tie the plaid ribbon around the neck for a scarf. Glue the black felt feet to the flat bottom. Fill the hat with candy, and you are ready for visitors.

Panoramic Ball with Music Box
(SEE COLOR INSERT)

Materials

8" panoramic Styrofoam ball	1" x 1" white felt
2 Christmas napkins with poinsettia and holly designs	1¾ yd red string beads
	5" pink yarn
6 Joan Walsh Anglund design Christmas Cards, 2 of each design	Music box with key
	Tiny red holly berries
	Red plastic glitter pins
3 miniature plastic kittens	Green plastic grass
2 miniature plastic bears	Gold glitter
6" bristle tree	Diamond dust
3" bristle tree	Mod Podge®
Two ½" plastic curtain rings	Decoupage or manicure scissors
1¾ yd of ½" gold braid	Hat pin
6" of ⅛" red satin ribbon	Straight pins
5 yd of ¼" red velvet ribbon	Silicone sealer
3" x 3" red felt	White glue

The cards I used were prints of interior Christmas scenes. Two of each of the three scenes were selected for three of the four openings. You may wish to use the greeting from inside a card for the fourth opening. For each of the scenes, cut one card to snugly fit the opening. The second, identical card is then cut out for overlaying the first card to give a three-dimensional depth to the scene.

If the Christmas cards used here are not available in your area, do not give up; the idea is great, so look for other cards or prints that can be used and do your own thing. Be creative.

CUTTING CARDS

Using card set no. 1, close a card and cut out a circle to fit the panoramic ball. You will have two circles, one from the front and one from the inside of the card. Glue the circles together to make a firmer circle. Let dry. Repeat this step on the other two cards. Select a greeting from the second set of cards. I chose "Happy Holidays." Using a previously cut circle as a pattern, center the circle over the greeting and draw around the pattern carefully with a pencil. Cut out. Do this on two cards and glue the circles together and let dry.

INSERTING THE MUSIC BOX

Carefully slice off approximately a 2-inch diameter slice from the bottom of the ball with a serrated knife. Save the slice. Next, place the music box over this sliced, flat area and trace around the music box with a pencil. With a knife or grapefruit spoon, scoop out the area inside the pencil markings just enough so that the music box will set inside the area and yet deep enough so the slice can be glued over the box at the same level as before. Glue the music box inside the cavity with white glue—remember, the keyhole should be on the outside.

After gluing the slice over the music box, make a hole in the Styrofoam where the key will go. Screw the key through the opening in the slice. Set Styrofoam ball aside for at least 24 hours to dry before turning key. It is important to have a permanent bond of the Styrofoam and music box; because of the weight of the music box, it will be at the bottom of the ball while hanging.

Using card set no. 2, cut out the main details that are to be featured in each of the three circles with decoupage or manicure scissors. Hold scissors open at a 45° angle, feeding the print into the scissor blades.

Details of each card will be defined below.

CHILDREN-AROUND-THE-TREE CIRCLE

Cut out all the tree ornaments such as the star, the bead garland (in long stripes), the horse, the candles with the halos, and the balls. Cut the girl, the boy holding the package, the drum, and the packages. Discard the background material. Next spread a line of white glue on the halos of all the cutout candles and the candles on the outer edges of the tree. Also spread glue on the cutout star and on the star on the print. Sprinkle gold glitter on all the glued areas; shake off the excess glitter. Let dry.

Cut a bristle tree to the size of the tree on the card; use wire cutters to trim the stem from the bottom only and, if necessary, use scissors to trim the bristles. When tree is correct length, shear off one side of the tree to make a flat side. Glue the flat side of the tree directly over the tree on the card. Glue the cutout ornaments, the glittered candles, the garland, and the star on the tree.

Shape the girl cutout by placing the colored side of the print down on the palm of your hand and gently push the edges of the cutout with the flat of your fingernail. The edges will curve outwardly to give a depth to the figure. Treat the boy cutout the same way; but leave his package flat.

Glue the shaped girl cutout around the tree with a ¼-inch high dot of silicone sealer, matching the bow and the edge of the skirt to the card. Glue the boy's hair to the card and glue his body and the package with ¼-inch dots of silicone sealer. Use a ½-inch dot of silicone sealer to attach cutout packages to the circle print. Do not push cutouts down against the print; you want to have a raised look. With a dot of silicone, glue a plastic bear over the bear on the print. Set aside to dry undisturbed—lay face up so sealer will not flatten.

TREE-ON-THE-TABLE CIRCLE

Cut out the candles (with the halos) and the star from the tree; the tablecloth; the boy and girl together; the stockings and the candle with halo and leaves; and the window frame. Cut the blue area out of the window.

Spread a line of white glue on the halos of all the cutout candles and on the candle on the fireplace. Spread white glue on the star cutout and on the star on the print. Sprinkle gold glitter onto the glued areas; then shake off excess glitter. Let dry.

Shape the boy and girl cutout as you did the previous card.

Use the cutout of the tablecloth as a pattern; and trace and cut one from red felt. Then cut off the top oval of the paper tablecloth and glue it to the felt shape with white glue. Discard lower half of the paper tablecloth.

Use the cutout stockings as patterns on the red and white felt. Glue the felt stockings to the fireplace and discard paper stockings. Use a ⅛-inch high dot of sealer to attach candle with leaves to the top of the fireplace. Be sure not to flatten dot of sealer too much—just enough to create a natural look.

Attach the shaped boy and girl cutout directly over the prints with a few ½-inch dots of sealer. Attach the window frame directly over the print frame; but this time use a thin line of sealer at least ¼-inch high, being sure not to let sealer show past the sides of the frame. Let dry.

Prepare a small plastic ring, the size of the wreath, by coating it with white glue then dipping it in loose green grass. Shake off the excess grass. Let dry. When dry, glue two groups of tiny red berries on the green covered ring to resemble holly berries. Make a tiny bow from the narrow, red satin ribbon and attach to top of wreath with white glue. When completely dry, glue the wreath ring directly to the wreath on the print.

As previously described, cut a bristle tree to the size of the tree and shear off one side to make it flat. Glue the flat side of the tree directly over the tree on the print. Glue the glittered candles and the star on the tree.

Use a few dots of silicone sealer about ¼-inch high to attach the red felt table skirt to the print. The tree should look as though it is sitting on the tabletop. (Optional: add fringe to the bottom of the table skirt.) Glue a plastic kitten over the kitten on the print. Make a small yarn ball from a scrap of yarn and glue this on. Let dry.

OPENING-A-PACKAGE CIRCLE

Cut out the girl, the boy, the package, the ball, and the window frame; discard background material. Shape the girl and boy cutout as previously described. Shape the ball as round as possible. (Optional: cut out the ball from the circle print, then glue a marble into the hole to resemble a ball.) Shape the cutout package by creasing the straight side to achieve a squared look to the box.

Cut out the blue area from the cutout window frame. Glue the cutout frame directly over the print frame with a thin ¼-inch high dot of sealer—be sure the sealer does not show. Let dry.

Prepare a plastic curtain ring, with loose green grass as previously described. When dry, glue red berries in two groups of three on the green covered ring to resemble holly berries. When completely dry, glue green wreath directly to the wreath on the print. Let dry.

Glue a plastic bear on the print with white glue; then attach cutout package with sealer over the bear, placing the top on an angle away from the bear so it looks like the bear is sitting in the box.

Attach the shaped girl cutout directly over the print with ½-inch dots of sealer under the head and the body. Girl's hand should extend over the plastic bear as though she were pulling the bear out of the package.

Attach shaped boy with ½-inch dots of sealer directly over the print. Glue two plastic kittens on print with white glue directly over the kittens on the print. Set aside to dry completely.

FRAMING THE SCENES IN THE PANORAMIC BALL

Place one of the circle prints over an opening on the Styrofoam ball. The print should set at least ½ inch inside the ball. If the opening is too small, trace around the circle carefully with a pencil. Do this on all four openings.

Next firmly push down the Styrofoam area inside the pencil markings with your thumb or with the top of a spoon for at least a ½-inch depth all around.

You will now have a ledge on which to glue your circle prints inside the ball. Do this on all four openings. Try circle print in the openings to be sure you have pushed down evenly and equally on each opening.

DECORATING THE OUTSIDE OF THE PANORAMIC BALL

To decorate the outside of the ball, you will need two Christmas napkins with poinsettias and holly designs. One napkin will be used for the top, the other for the bottom of the ball.

Most napkins are either two or three-ply thickness. Separate the plys, pulling the top (decorated) layer away from the other layer. Use only the top layer, the other can be saved for cleanup. Do this to both napkins.

With scissors, cut out the flowers, the holly, and the berries from the napkin. It is not important to cut away the white area, because this will blend into the Styrofoam. A flower design can be placed in the corners or above the openings in a pleasing design.

When a design has been determined, brush the top of the ball with a coat of Mod Podge. Place the flowers into the Mod Podge, using the brush to flatten out the napkin and removing the wrinkles which may occur. Repeat on the bottom of the ball.

Be sure to place a flower design on the slice over the music box, being careful not to get Mod Podge in the keyhole. Also place holly and berry designs between the openings.

Next, brush a medium coat of Mod Podge over the entire Styrofoam ball, except for the pushed in ledge in the four openings. Sprinkle diamond dust over the Mod Podge coating while holding the ball over a clean sheet of paper to catch the excess diamond dust. Shake off excess. Let dry for at least one hour.

After the one hour drying time, you will then push the red plastic glitter pins into the berry design on the ball. Scatter the pins evenly over the entire ball except for the berries that may be on the posts between the openings. Let dry completely.

Cut two pieces of red velvet ribbon 26 inches in length and one piece 12 inches in length. Place one end of the 26-inch length of velvet ribbon at the top of the ball, then down between two openings, across the bottom, up between two openings on the opposite side to the top. The other 26-inch velvet ribbon will be wrapped around the opposite direction, crossing the first ribbon on the bottom. Glue the ribbon in place with white glue.

Make a full-looped bow with the remaining velvet ribbon, gluing the center of this bow to the top of the ball where the 26-inch ribbon lengths meet. For extra security, place several straight pins in the loops at the center and a large hat pin in the center of the bow.

To make a loop to hang the ball, use a 12-inch ribbon or braid. Glue the ends together and then place at center of the bow, remove hat pin from the bow and replace with added glue. Let dry completely before trying to hang it up. For added length, you can use nylon thread through this 12-inch loop.

ASSEMBLING PRINTS IN OPENINGS

Spread a line of white glue on the ledge of the opening in the Styrofoam ball. Place the circle print carefully onto the glue. Be sure to place the scene straight on the ledge. Next spread white glue on the edge of the opening and place a 15-inch length of gold braid into the glue. Pins can be used to hold the braid in place while drying. Overlap braid slightly, trim. Spread a thin line of white glue on the center of the braid, then place a length of red plastic beads into the glue. Pins will help hold the beads in place while drying.

Do this to all four openings. Let dry and hang. Now stand back and enjoy your new Christmas decoration—after you have turned the key to the music box.

Door
&
Wall
Hangings

Chapter 3

Fringe Tree

Here's an idea to use up some of the pieces of ball fringe you may have left over from another project (Fig. 2-12).

Materials

21" x 34½" red burlap
8 yd of 1" green fringe
9 black fringe balls, 1" diam.
15 yellow fringe balls, ¾" diam.
6 white fringe balls, ¾" diam.
6 red fringe balls, ¾" diam.
5 pink fringe balls, ½" diam.

5 orange fringe balls, ½" diam.
4 red fringe balls, ½" diam.
20" of ⅜" wooden dowel
24" yellow cord
White glue
Wax paper

Along both 34½-inch sides and one 21-inch side, pull threads off the burlap to create a one-inch fringe around the three sides. Fold over 1½ inches on the unfringed side and glue along the edge. Insert the dowel into this slot. Tie one end of the yellow cord to each end of the dowel. Glue one ¾-inch red fringe ball over each end of the dowel to hide the knot in the cord.

44

Lay the burlap on wax paper. This will stop the glue from sticking to your craft table while you are "growing" your tree.

First, spread a row of glue 7 inches from the bottom and 2½ inches from each side, excluding the fringe, thus making a 14-inch line. Lay the selvage of the green fringe along this line. Then fold the fringe at the end of this row to start the next row. Each row should be ¼ inch shorter on each side than the preceding row and ¼ inch above the preceding row. The tree, excluding the star, will be 18 inches high and the top will come to a point.

To make the star, use one yellow fringe ball as the center at the point of the tree. Then, use two yellow balls for each point of the star. Glue in place.

For the decorations on the tree, scatter the ¾-inch balls on the lower half of the tree and the smaller balls on the top portion. For the trunk of the tree, arrange and glue the nine black fringe balls into a square.

When all the glue has dried, peel the wax paper off the back of the burlap and hang it up by the yellow cord.

Bells and Bows

(SEE FRONT COVER)

'Tis nice to hear a jingle when people visit at holiday time, so your Bells and Bows will be well suited on your entrance door. You can also try this idea using burlap, polka dot, or calico ribbon.

Materials

27" of 4" red, water-repellent, velvet-like ribbon	1 yd #28 wire
3½ yd of 1½" plaid ribbon	Gold 2" ring
5 gold metal bells	White glue
2 red chenille stems	Pencil

So that you do not crease the ribbon, gently fold one end of red ribbon in half lengthwise. Start at the edge, 3 inches from end, cut a 45° angle toward the center, making a V-shaped cut. This method gives you a balanced cut. Unfold the ribbon. Using the same method, cut a point on one end of the plaid ribbon.

On the back of the red ribbon, put white glue on all edges, except the point. Keeping the points of both ribbons even, lay the center of the plaid ribbon into the glue. The plaid ribbon is attached on the wrong side of the ribbon but extends over the edge of the red ribbon and, thus, forms a border of plaid ribbon. Continue gluing the plaid ribbon around the red ribbon. Let dry.

With a pencil, make a mark on the back in the center of the ribbon every 4½ inches. Make two small slits with the point of your scissors at these five places.

You will need five 12-inch pieces of plaid ribbon to make the bows. Cut a point on both ends of all five pieces. Make five single loop bows and use a piece of wire to secure each bow. Cut off any excess wire.

Cut five 4-inch pieces of chenille stems. Push a chenille stem through the loop in top of the bell. Wrap the chenille stem around center of bow. Twist once to secure it. On the front of the red ribbon, push the chenille stem ends through the holes. Twist at the back of the red ribbon. Do the same with the other chenille stems.

Cut a 6-inch piece of plaid ribbon. Run it through the gold ring and glue both ends to center top for hanging. Let dry.

White Branch a'Hanging
(SEE COLOR INSERT)

Sometimes it is fun to use colors other than the traditional ones for Christmas. We made this hanging for our pink bathroom. The silver trim complements the blue, but if you prefer gold—use it! Remember, in crafts, substitution is fine and many times necessary.

Materials

12″ x 18″ royal blue felt	1 package 4mm pearls
2″ x 4″ hot pink felt	12 hot pink spoke sequins
2 yd silver braid	1 package hot pink 5mm sequins
½ yd silver cord	Diamond dust
13″ ¼″ wooden dowel	Flat white plastic branch
12″ x 18″ piece wax paper	White glue
60″ strand 2mm pearls	Toothpick

Along one of the 12-inch sides, fold down 1½ inches and glue, making sure to leave enough room to slide the dowel in. Turn the felt over to glue the silver braid along all four edges. Spread a thin line of white glue just inside the braid. Place the strand of pearls on this line. You will have some pearls left over to use later. Let it dry.

Cover the branch with a thin layer of glue and sprinkle diamond dust on it. While this is drying, cut the pink felt into the shape of a simple planter, with a bottom of 2 inches and a top of 4 inches. Glue a 4-inch piece of silver braid at the top.

Now the branch is ready to work with again. Spread a thin layer of glue on the back of the branch and position it in the center of the blue felt. To secure the branch to the felt, place the wax paper over the branch and set a heavy book on it for a few minutes.

Remove the book and wax paper to start decorating your tree. With a toothpick, put glue on the back of the sequins and place at random. Then, glue a 4 mm pearl in the center of each spoke sequin and the 2 mm pearls in the center of the smaller sequins.

Now that your planter is dry, glue it at the base of the tree. Put the dowel in the slot at the top. Tie one end of the cord to either end of the dowel for hanging.

Joy

This wall hanging (Fig. 2-9) was made for a neighbor's front hallway. Her colors are gold and turquoise, so this wall hanging blended in very well. The hanging can be done in any color combination.

Materials

14″ x 16″ turquoise felt	2 blue beads
18″ x 24″ yellow felt	2 gold bell caps
2½ yd of ½″ gold and turquoise braid	3 straight pins
	Gold paint
1¾ yd of ¾″ gold ladder braid	Brush
3⅓ yd of ¹⁄₁₆″ gold flat braid	White glue
20″ of ¼″ wood dowel	

Fold over 2 inches of the 18-inch end of the yellow felt. Spread white glue on the edge of the folded felt and press against the felt. This is the top of the hanging and will form a hem for inserting the dowel. Paint 3 inches of each end of the wooden dowel gold, and set aside to dry.

Cut an angel and the letters J-O-Y from the turquoise felt, following the pattern outlines in Figs. 3-1 and 3-2.

On the left side of the yellow felt, measure down 7½ inches from the top and 3½ inches in from the side. Mark this point with a straight pin. This point is where the tip of the angel's left wing will be

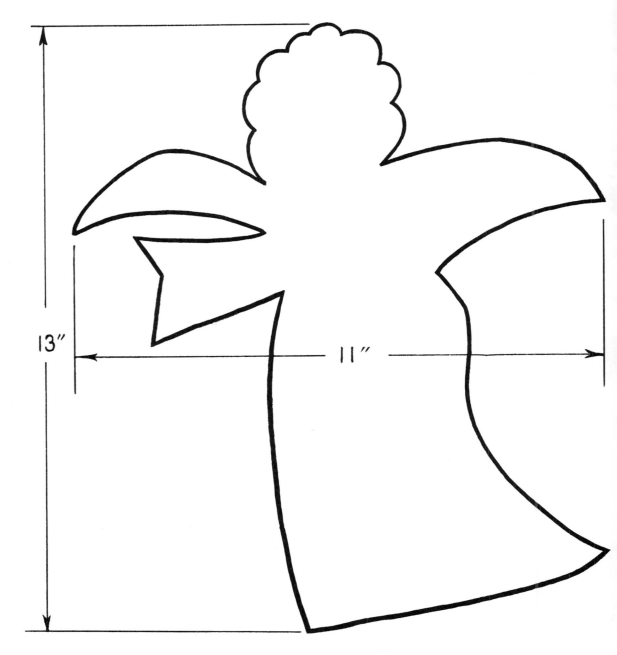

Fig. 3-1 Angel pattern. This pattern has been reduced: 1″ = 2″

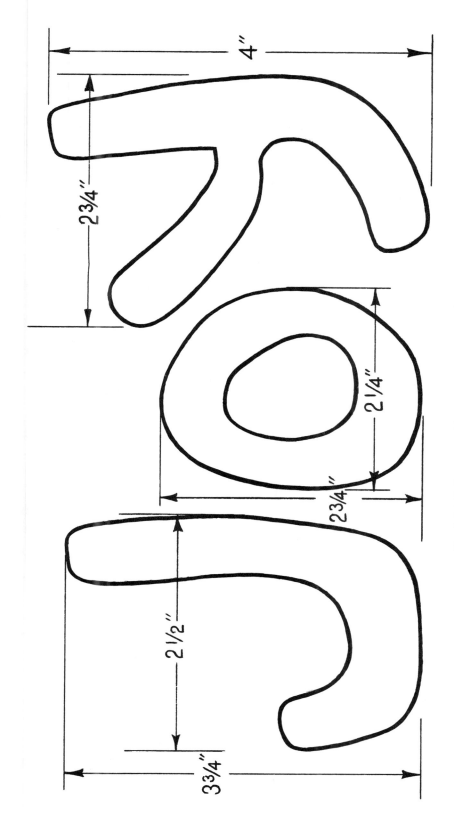

Fig. 3-2 J-O-Y patterns. These patterns are actual size.

positioned. On the right side of the yellow felt, measure down 5½ inches from the top and 3½ inches in from the side. Mark this point with a pin. This is the position for the point of the angel's right wing.

50

Spread glue on the back-side edges of the turquoise angel. Turn the angel over and place the wing tips at the marked positions. The angel's head should be 2 inches from the top, and the right tip of the skirt should be 2 inches from the edge of the felt. Be careful not to smear the glue while gluing the angel to the yellow felt. If you get glue where it shouldn't be, dampen a cloth and carefully wipe it off.

Starting at the neckline of the angel, glue the gold ladder braid all around the edge of the angel. Be careful turning the corner and curves. You may have to cut the braid to have it lay smoothly. If so, butt the cut ends together and then glue them so that they will not ravel. Glue flat gold braid around the head.

Next, glue the letter J on the left side of the angel, 2 inches below the tip of the left wing and 3 inches in from the edge of the yellow felt. Tilt the J just a little. The O is glued one inch below the J. Glue the Y slightly to the right. Trim the letters by gluing the ¹/₁₆-inch gold braid around the edges and at the center of each letter.

Starting at a corner of the yellow felt, spread glue all around the edge. Lay the ½-inch gold and turquoise braid into the glue. Turn the corners carefully. Push the wood dowel through the top hem. Glue a bell cap on each end of the dowel. Next glue a blue bead in the center of each bell cap. Spread glue on the dowel just to the inside of the bell cap. Lay one end of the flat gold braid in the glue, wrap 1½ inches of braid around the dowel. Glue the other end of the gold braid on the dowel in the same manner. Your banner is ready for hanging.

Angel on a Mat
(SEE BACK COVER)

The mat that is used for the base of this creation can be found in most craft stores. If you prefer, you may find an oval place mat in its natural color. Either way, you will create a lovely wall hanging.

Materials

13″ x 18″ natural color mat
2 yd of ¾″ gold braid
24″ of 4″ red, water-repellent,
    satin-back ribbon
7 plastic holly picks

24″ #28 wire
3 fern pins
Plastic flat back gold angel
White glue

Starting at one of the shorter sides on the mat, glue the gold braid around the edges.

Cut off 4 inches of the ribbon. This will be the tie in the center of the bow. Cut a triangular piece out of each end of the 20 inches of ribbon. Gather the ribbon in the center and wrap the 4 inches of ribbon folded in half lengthwise around the gathering, and glue it in place. Then at the end of the mat, where you started gluing the braid, glue the bow over the two ends of braid in order to hide the seam.

While this dries, cut off 4 inches of the wire and set it aside. Group four of the holly picks like you would hold a bouquet and wrap wire around the stems. Pull tightly, but do not cut off the remaining wire. Now, group the three remaining holly picks together and lay their stems in the opposite direction on top of the other stems. Wrap the wire around the whole bunch of stems, tightly securing them together. Lay the bunch of holly slightly to the left of center under the bow. This is the top of the mat. With one fern pin, place it over the stems and push it through the mat. Twist the two ends together at the back of the mat. Do the same with the other fern pins placing one under each bunch of holly.

With the 4 inches of wire left, make a hanger by pushing it through the mat behind the bow. Glue the angel about 3 inches from the bottom of the mat. Let all the glue dry before hanging up your new creation.

Kitchen Door

I needed a decoration for our kitchen door. Our old grater was due to be replaced so this decoration grew from that. Looking through my collection of craft supplies this is what I came up with (Fig. 7-6). After Christmas I moved it from the door to the kitchen wall. It's such a cheerful item I couldn't put it away. Have fun!

Materials

16″ diam. rattan mat	6 white chenille stems
2½ yd of 3″ yellow print ribbon	½ yd #28 wire
12 plastic vegetable picks	Kitchen grater
4″ x 4″ Styrofoam block	White glue
6 red berry picks	Red spray paint

Spray the grater red and set it aside to dry.

Run the yellow print ribbon through the open work of the rattan mat. Cut and glue the ends together.

Center the painted grater on the rattan mat. Cut a 6-inch length of chenille stem. Push it through the holes in the back of the grater and then through the mat. Twist ends together in back.

Cut the Styrofoam to fit inside grater and push inside the grater. Push plastic vegetables into Styrofoam, arranging as you go. Keep the scallions for the front, attach them to the grater with a 4-inch piece of chenille stem. Stick four of the red berry picks among the green vegetables.

Cut two 27-inch pieces of yellow print ribbon. Make a single loop bow from both pieces. Use the wire to attach bows to mat near bottom of the grater, laying the bows sideways. Glue one bunch of red berries to the center of each bow.

I used the bottom of the grater as the top of my decoration. So, cut a piece of chenille stem 6 inches long. Push through mat just above the handle and twist ends on back of mat. Use this for hanging your decoration.

Kiddies' Treasure

(SEE FRONT COVER)

The first of December to Christmas is the longest time of the year.
It seems as though ole' Santa Claus never will appear.
How many more days till Christmas? It's mighty hard to count.
So this candy hanging will tell you the exact amount.
Untie one ribbon every night and have a candy please.
And when you reach the bell, it will be Christmas Eve!
Merry Christmas

Materials

30" chair webbing	Large eye needle
6 yd red yarn	Plastic bell
24 pieces mixed wrapped candy	

Fold webbing in half lengthwise. At one end, starting at end on the centerfold, stitch at 45° angle over to edge. Trim off excess webbing. Turn inside out. Glue the plastic bell to point.

Thread the needle with yarn about 24 inches long. In center of webbing, 2 inches above the bell, stitch through webbing from the front. Then stitch through from back to front, leaving 4-inch tails on each end. Lay one end of wrapped candy paper over yarn and tie a bow with the yarn.

Continue this pattern 1½ inches above the first candy at a 45° angle, 1½ inches in from edge.

Repeat until you've used your twenty-four pieces of candy.

Use a 12-inch piece of yarn, and sew through the top of webbing. Tie into a bow for hanging.

Jolly Santa
(SEE COLOR INSERT)

There are many rattan shapes available. This is one of my favorites. A friend made this for me.

Materials

Santa rattan frame	14″ x 20″ green felt
7 yd white velvet tubing	9 white ball fringe pompoms, 1″ diam.
5 yd red velvet tubing	White glue

Lay the rattan frame over the green felt. Draw an outline with a pencil. Remove frame and cut out the felt. Spread glue on the back of the outside edges and on the back of the moustache part of the rattan. Lay the rattan on top of the green felt shape and press firmly. Be sure the edges match evenly. Trim off any excess felt.

Very carefully put glue on frame outline of hat and the top and bottom of the hatband. Lay the red tubing into the glue and cut the tubing to fit. Apply glue to ends of tubing and pinch together. This will keep the tubing ends from raveling. Also glue red tubing for the upper lip of the mouth.

Glue white tubing to the rest of the rattan frame. Be very careful not to get the glue on the front of the tubing. For the eyes, wind the tubing around and around to make a circle. On the whiskers, overlap the tubing and cut only at each end.

Glue the nine 1-inch ball fringe pompoms to each other in a circle. Place at the tip of Santa's hat and fasten with glue.

On back of the green felt, glue a loop of white tubing for hanging your new Christmas decoration.

Mittens for Your Door
(SEE COLOR INSERT)

This has always been a favorite doorpiece of mine. It is inexpensive and very quick to assemble. It makes a nice gift for a neighbor or donation to a bazaar.

Materials

12" x 18" red felt	Four 12" lengths #28 wire
1 yd white yarn	18" x 24" branch of evergreens
Two 2" Styrofoam balls	Poster board
2 yd of 1⅜" red, water-repellent, velvet-type ribbon	White glue

54

Cut two mitten shapes from the red felt (Fig. 3-3). On one mitten shape, apply glue to all but the wrist edges. Lay the glued side on the uncut felt. Let it dry and then cut around it and you'll have your first mitten. This is the best way to get the edges to match. Repeat this procedure to make your second mitten.

Now, cut the yarn in half and tie a bow with each half. Glue one bow to each wrist. Then glue a Styrofoam ball to each palm of the mittens to give the effect of snowballs.

In the untrimmed half of each mitten, make two small holes in the palm. Thread the holes in each mitten with one piece of wire. With the cut end of the branch at the top, use the wire to attach the mittens to the center of the greens.

Make a bow from the red ribbon. Position it near the top of the greens, using the wire to secure it. Wrap a piece of wire on the branch just above the bow and make a loop for hanging.

Hallway Holly

(SEE COLOR INSERT)

Rattan mats can be found in several sizes. They are available in many colors; the natural colored ones can be spray painted.

Materials

16" red rattan mat	Red chenille stem
4" x 4" x 2" Styrofoam block	2 green chenille stems
12 plastic holly picks	2 yd of 2" wide red velvet ribbon

Lay the Styrofoam block in the center of the rattan mat. Bend one green chenille stem into a U shape. Push the two loose ends through the Styrofoam and through the rattan mat. Twist the two ends together in order to secure the Styrofoam to the mat.

Cut the plastic holly picks to 4 inches in length. Insert the picks on the four sides of the Styrofoam block first; then fill in the center of the Styrofoam.

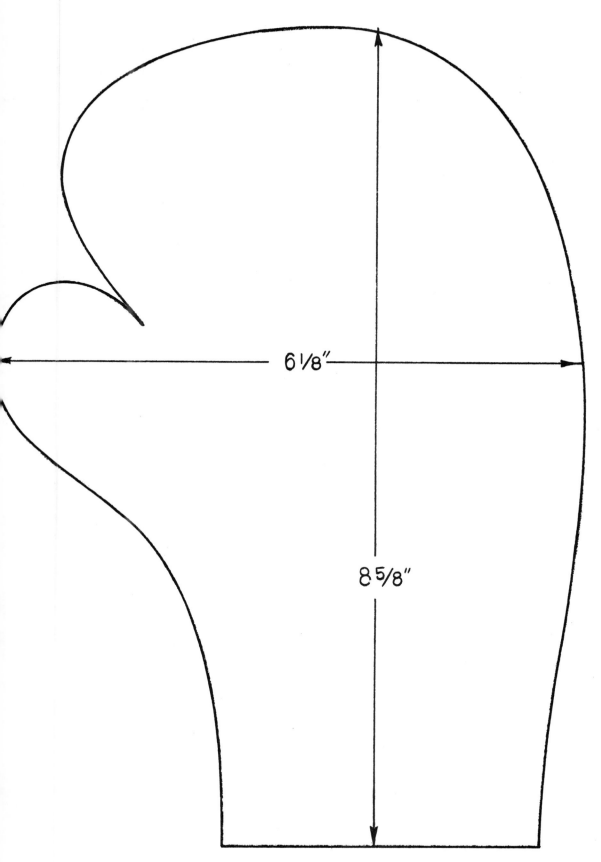

6 1/8"

8 5/8"

Fig. 3-3 Mitten pattern. This pattern is actual size.

Make a bow from the red ribbon and secure the center with the red chenille stem. To attach the bow below the holly, push the chenille stem through the mat and twist the ends together. Use the other green chenille stem to form a hook at the top, on the back of the mat.

This decoration can be varied by using permanent fruits, small pixies, tiny angels, or even a few real pine cones.

Wreaths

$$Chapter$$
$$4$$

Chenille Wreath

Materials

12" diam., 1½" wide
Styrofoam flat ring
12 yd of 3" green bump chenille

3½ yd of 3" red bump chenille
4" #28 wire
White glue

The finished Chenille Wreath is pictured in Fig. 4-1.

Cut forty pieces of the green bump chenille with two bumps in each piece. With one pair of bumps, fold the section in half where the chenille is the thinnest and pinch the fold. Do this for all forty pairs of green chenille. Put glue on the two loose ends of a pair of bumps. Keeping these ends together, push them into the ring one inch from the edge (Fig. 4-1). Continue for each pair and place them ¾ inch from each other.

Cut the remaining green bumps into single pieces. Wrap each one around your finger to make curlicues. With glue on one end of the curl, push it into the ring at the inside edge and flatten the curl in order

Fig. 4-1 Chenille Wreath, Christmas Song Book, Mushroom Tree.

to cover the end of the pair of bumps. Continue around the inside edge.

Cut a section of four red bumps, leaving them connected. Cut the rest of the red chenille into single bumps. Twist the single bumps into curlicues. With glue on one end of the curls, push these into the inside rim of the Styrofoam.

With the four red bumps that are connected, make a bow. Make a loop from the two bumps in the center. Twist one of the end bumps around the center. Put wire around center and use it to secure the bow by pushing it into the Styrofoam. Shape the loops and the two loose ends into a pretty bow.

With a leftover chenille bump, make a loop for hanging. Put glue on the loose ends and push it into the back of the Styrofoam opposite the bow.

This wreath is pretty in other colors and combinations—maybe to match your decor. Have fun!

60

Yarn Wreath

(SEE COLOR INSERT)

Materials

Six 70 yd skeins heavy rug yarn,
    2 blue, 2 green, 2 purple
22″ Styrofoam ring
    covered with green plastic
66 fern pins

3 bunches plastic grapes,
    1 blue, 1 green, 1 purple
2 yd of 1⅜″ green, water-repellent,
    velvet-type ribbon
Eight 12″ lengths #28 wire
3″ x 4″ heavy cardboard

Cut each skein of yarn into 6-yard lengths. Cut twenty-two 4-inch pieces from the left over yarn in each color.

Use the 3-inch by 4-inch cardboard to form pompoms. Wrap one 6-yard length of yarn around the 4-inch length of cardboard. Slip one matching 4-inch piece of yarn underneath the loop at the edge of the cardboard. Pull it tightly around the loop and tie a knot. Place a second 4-inch piece at the opposite side of loop and tie a knot. Cut the yarn loop in the center between the knots on both sides of cardboard forming two pompoms (Fig. 4-2).

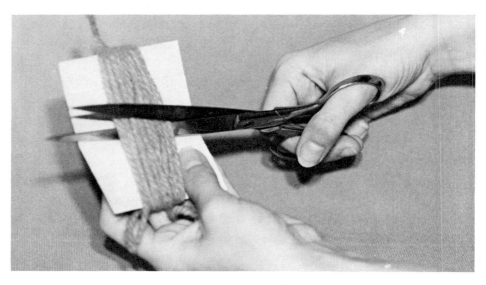

Fig. 4-2 Cutting yarn loop.

Fig. 4-3 Placing fern pin.

Lay one pompom crossed over the other. Using the tie piece on the top pompom, tie the two pompoms together. Slip a fern pin through the tie loop (Fig. 4-3). Fluff the double pompom into a puff. Continue tying until twenty-two of each color have been formed.

Assemble the wreath by pushing the fern pins into the Styrofoam ring (Fig. 4-4). Place the three colors of pompoms alternately to cover the ring. Do not place pompoms on the back of the ring.

Fig. 4-4 Placing pompom on ring.

Visually divide the ring into quarters. Place a bunch of grapes at the top and side quarter points. Use the lengths of wire to fasten the grapes to the wreath, pushing one piece of wire through the grapes at the top and another at the bottom. Wrap the wire around the ring, and twist the ends to secure the bunches.

Form a bow from the green velvet ribbon. Fasten the bow at the bottom quarter of the wreath, with wire. Wrap the last length of wire around the ring at the top and make a loop for hanging.

Bows' Delight

Materials

18" straw ring	2⅓ yd of 1½" wide
3¼ yd of 1½" wide	pink and orange plaid ribbon
pink polka dot ribbon	2 pink straw birds
2⅓ yd of 1½" wide	White chenille stem
purple and white gingham	4 straight pins
ribbon	#28 wire

Cut nine 12-inch pieces of #28 wire. Cut the gingham and plaid ribbon material into three pieces, each 27 inches long. Cut two 27-inch pieces from the polka dot ribbon. Cut the ends of each ribbon piece at a 45-degree angle. Form these eight ribbon pieces into double loop bows. Wrap the wire around the center of the bow, and twist the wire tightly. Do not cut off the excess wire.

Form a double loop bow from the remaining polka dot ribbon, leaving 18-inch streamers on each side. Wrap wire around the center of the bow, and twist the wire tightly. Lay the bow on the straw ring and wrap the remaining length of the tie wire around the ring. Twist the wire tightly on the back side of the ring, and cut off any extra length of wire. This bow marks the top center of the ring.

Bring the bow streamers down at an angle, to form an inverted "v". Attach the ends of the streamers to the straw ring with two straight pins.

Space the eight remaining bows evenly around the ring, alternating designs. Start with a plaid bow to the right of the polka dot bow already on the ring. Attach the bows by wrapping the tie wires around the ring and twisting the wire at the back. Cut off any extra wire.

Fasten the straw birds at the bottom center of the ring by pushing

Fig. 4-5 Dried Flowers, Tinsel Tree Painting, Bows' Delight.

their mounting picks into the ring. Wrap a length of wire around the top of the ring for a hanger.

Your new straw wreath (Fig. 4-5) is now ready to greet holiday visitors.

Dried Flower Wreath

Materials

12″ straw ring
5 yd of ½″ blue velvet ribbon
4 wheat stalks
6 large strawflowers
Dried hydrangea blossoms
Assorted dried flowers
2 dozen fern pins

Cut a 12-inch length of blue velvet ribbon. Wrap it around the straw ring once and tie ends of streamers together into a knot. With the knot of the ribbon hanging down away from the ring, push a fern pin through the center of the ribbon into the straw ring. This will be the top center of your wreath.

Lay two stalks of wheat on each side of the ribbon, placing the heads of the stalks 3 inches from the ribbon, extending the ends over the edge of the straw ring. Hold the stalks in place by pushing fern pins over the stems firmly into the straw ring.

Directly on top of the velvet ribbon, secure one large strawflower by pushing its wire stem into the straw ring. Now secure two straw-flowers on each side of the first one. Fill in around and over to the heads of the wheat with hydrangea blossoms and the assorted dried flowers. Secure each piece of dried flower with a fern pin.

Make a triple bow with 2½ yards of ribbon. Attach at center top of the wreath with a fern pin.

Now make a double bow from remaining blue velvet ribbon. Place it at the bottom center of the ring and secure with a fern pin. Place one large strawflower over center of the bow. Arrange the remaining dried flowers around the top of this bow, securing each piece with a fern pin.

This is a good wreath (Fig. 4-5) to display anytime of the year.

Thread Cone Wreath

Materials

20 thread cones	2 plastic holly leaf picks
20 round wooden clothespins	4 plastic pine picks
20 red Christmas balls, 1½" diameter	4 plastic cedar picks
	3" x 3" x 1" green Styrofoam
3 yd of 3" wide red and white gingham ribbon	2 green chenille stems
	White chenille stem
7 Styrofoam balls, ½" diameter	Gold spray paint
White dove	White glue
4 white plastic branches	Floral adhesive
6 plastic holly berry picks	Heavy cardboard

This is a great idea for using thread cones (Fig. 4-6). They are readily available if you live near a garment factory, or they may be purchased from a craft shop.

Arrange the thread cones in a circle, laying them side by side with the big ends to the outside. Use the clothespins to pin the cones together from the outer edge of the circle. Place a dab of glue inside each clothespin before pinning the cones.

Cut an 8-inch diameter cardboard circle. Spread glue over one side of the cardboard circle. Lay the cone ring on the cardboard, being certain that the cardboard circle is in the center of the ring.

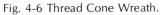
Fig. 4-6 Thread Cone Wreath.

Allow the glue to dry. The cardboard is kept to the back side of the wreath.

In preparation for spraying paint, spread newspaper over your work area. Lay the cone ring on the newspapers. Spray the cone ring with gold paint. Allow one side to dry before turning over to spray paint the other side. Be sure to spray paint the inside of all the cones. Allow the paint to dry.

Put a small piece of floral adhesive on one side of the Styrofoam block and stick it to the center of the cone ring. Push two white plastic branches into one edge of the Styrofoam block, the outside ends of the branches should be about one inch from the outer edge of the ring. Push the other two white plastic branches into the opposite edge of the Styrofoam block.

Now place the holly berry picks on the Styrofoam block, push two picks into each side and two picks into the top center of the block. Arrange the pine and cedar picks over the front of the Styrofoam, pushing them into place. Place the two holly leaf picks in the midst of all the greens. Set the white dove just above the holly leaves, and push the mounting pick into the Styrofoam.

Cut seven 3-inch pieces of green chenille stem. Insert a piece of chenille stem in each Styrofoam ball. Group the balls just a little to the left of the center of the Styrofoam block and push the stems into the block.

Make a double loop bow from the red and white gingham ribbon. Wrap a 6-inch piece of white chenille stem around the center of the bow and twist tightly in back. Mount the bow at the bottom center of the Styrofoam block by pushing the chenille stem into the block.

Spread glue on the hanger of each red Christmas ball. Place the hanger into the middle, open part of the clothespins. Glue a Christmas ball onto each clothespin. Make a loop hanger from the remaining piece of chenille stem. Glue the loop on the back side of the cone ring at the top center. Let the glue dry.

Your thread cone wreath is ready for display at your next club meeting.

Satin
People
Ornaments

Chapter

5

The satin balls you purchase may have a plastic hook for a hanger, or they may have a chenille stem, or they may have no hanger at all. These directions are written for the larger satin balls with plastic hooks and the smaller balls with chenille stems.

If the satin balls you purchase are not like this, use the following directions. When it is time to mount the head, use a 2-inch length of chenille stem for the neck. Put glue on the piece of stem and push it into the ball one inch. If the directions call for a plastic hook for the hanger, you may use a needle to sew a stitch with the cord to make the hanger. Now have fun making your satin Christmas people.

Full-size pattern pieces A to V are given in Fig. 5-1 for all parts needed to make these satin people ornaments.

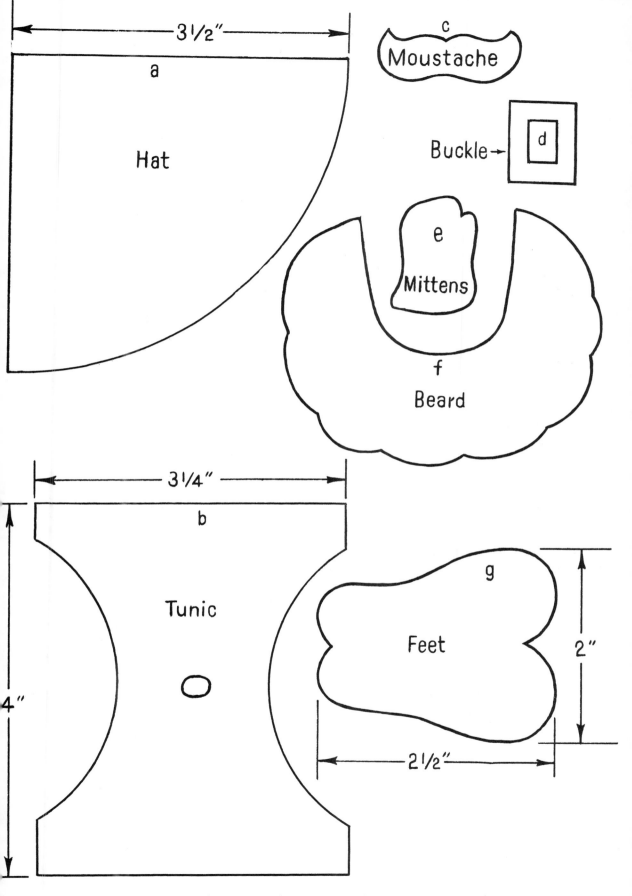

Fig. 5-1 Patterns A to V for Satin People Ornaments. These patterns are actual size.

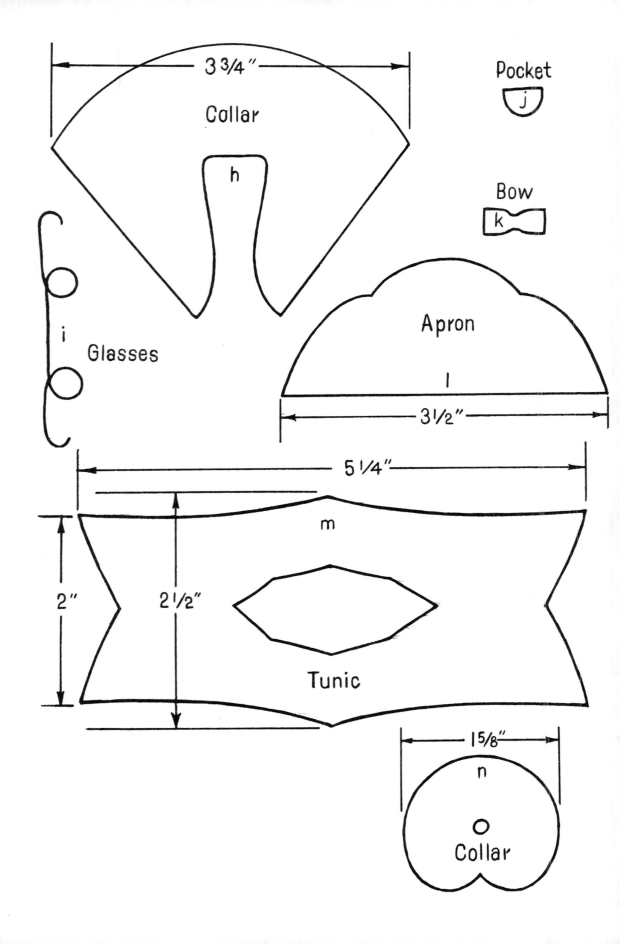

3 3/4"

Collar

h

Pocket

j

Bow

k

i

Glasses

Apron

l

3 1/2"

5 1/4"

m

2"

2 1/2"

Tunic

1 5/8"

n

Collar

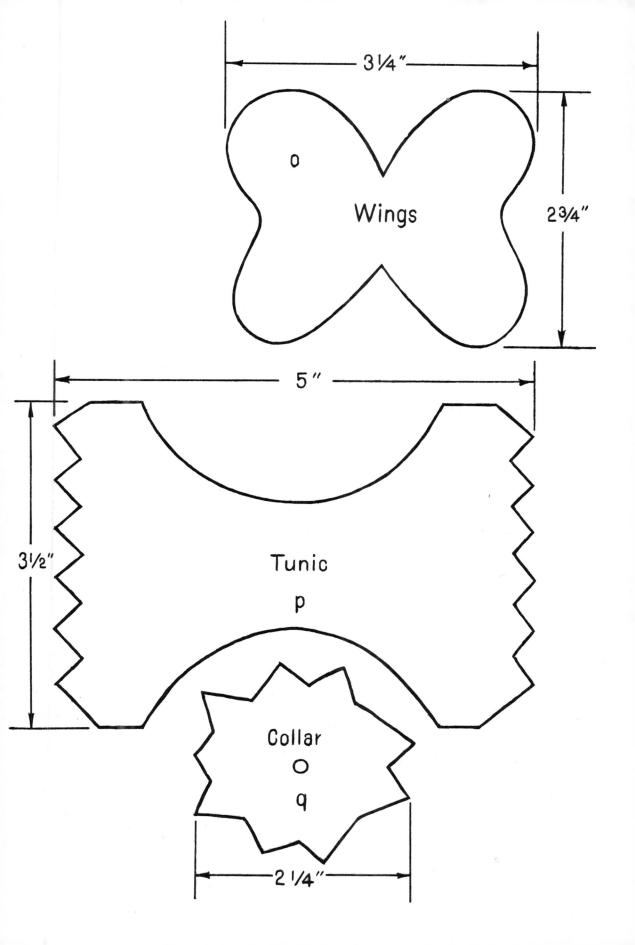

3¼"

2¾"

o

Wings

5"

3½"

Tunic

p

Collar

O

q

2¼"

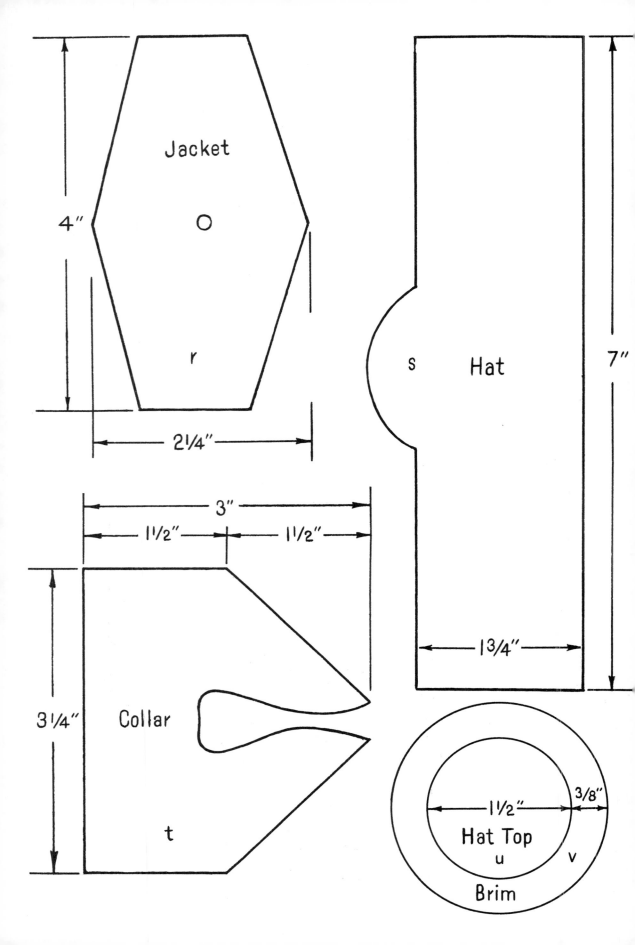

Jacket

4"

O

r

2¼"

Hat

s

7"

1¾"

3"

1½" 1½"

Collar

3¼"

t

1½"

3/8"

Hat Top

u   v

Brim

Santa Claus

(SEE COLOR INSERT)

Materials

Here are the materials and patterns needed for this project.

4″ x 7″ red felt; cut one A, one B, and one ¼″ dot	2″ pink satin ball
	2½″ red satin ball
4″ x 9″ white felt; cut one C, two E, and one F	½″ white fringe ball
	8″ gold cord
3″ x 5″ black felt; cut two G	Two 7mm wiggle eyes
1″ x 1″ gold felt; cut one D	Needle with large eye
¼″ x ¼″ pink felt; cut one ¼″ dot	White glitter
3″ x 3″ poster board; cut one G	White glue

Also, cut out the following dimensional strip pieces.

1″ x 5″ white felt strip, for hat trim	Two ¾″ x 3¼″ white felt strips, for tunic trim
	½″ x 1½″ black felt strip, for belt

Place a thin line of glue along the edges of both of the ¾ by 3¼-inch white felt tunic trim pieces, and sprinkle white glitter on the glue. Now lay the red felt tunic on a flat surface. Glue the tunic trim pieces on the straight edges of the tunic. Glue the ½ by 1½-inch black felt belt above one of the tunic trims. This will be the front of the Santa. The gold felt belt buckle is then glued in the center on top of the belt. Place a thin line of glue on the cuffs of the mittens and sprinkle with glitter. Glue the mittens on the tunic at either end of the belt.

Glue one black felt foot on each side of the poster board feet. Set aside to dry. Remove the plastic hook from the red satin ball. Place the small hole in the tunic over the hole in the red ball. Glue the front and back of the tunic so that it hugs the red ball. Now glue the feet to the bottom of the ball.

Use the chenille stem on the pink satin ball as the neck. Holding the chenille stem, use a finger to spread glue around the top and sides of the pink ball to resemble a hairline. Sprinkle white glitter onto the wet glue. When this dries, apply glue along the U-shaped edge of the white felt beard. Put the beard in place on the pink ball to frame

Santa's face. Glue the small red dot at the edge of the beard for his mouth. Glue the white felt moustache above the mouth so that the ends of Santa's moustache touch his beard. Now glue the pink felt dot above the moustache for Santa's nose. To finish his face, glue the wiggle eyes in place.

Place a thin line of glue on one straight edge of the red felt hat. Form the hat into a cone shape and press the glued edge onto the other straight edge. Do not overlap the seam too much. Try the hat on the pink ball for a fit, let it dry on the ball and then remove the hat. Spread a thin line of glue along the edges of the white felt hat trim and sprinkle glitter on the wet glue. Glue one long edge of the hat trim onto the brim of the hat, being sure the trim meets in the back. Place a line of glue around the inside brim of the hat and then place it on Santa's head. Be sure to cover the ends of his beard. Glue down the tip of the hat to one side. Glue the white fringe ball on the tip of the hat.

Dip the end of the chenille stem on the pink ball into the glue and push the stem into the hole on top of the red ball. Thread the needle with gold cord and push the needle through the fold at the top of the hat. Tie the ends of the cord together to make a hanger.

Mrs. Claus
(SEE COLOR INSERT)

Materials

Here are the materials and patterns needed for this project.

8″ x 8″ red felt; cut one H, one J, one 4″ circle, and one ¼″ dot	2″ pink satin ball
10″ x 3″ white felt; cut two E, one J, one K, and two ¼″ dots	2½″ red satin ball
	6″ #28 wire
	5 straight pins
3″ x 5″ black felt; cut two G	Silver glitter
¼″ x ¼″ pink felt; cut one ¼″ dot	Needle with large eye
3″ x 3″ poster board; cut one G	Red thread
8″ gold cord	White glue
Two 7mm wiggle eyes	

Also, cut out the following dimensional strip pieces from the white felt.

Two ½″ x 2½″ collar trim	½″ x 7″ bonnet trim
½″ x 4¼″ collar trim	½″ x 10″ apron string

Lay the red felt collar on a flat surface. Glue the two shortest collar trim white felt strips on the straight edges of the collar. Glue the longer collar trim white felt strip around the curve of the collar, easing in the fullness. Remove the plastic hook from the red satin ball. Place the collar close to the hole on top of the red ball. Secure the center and corners of the collar with glue.

Glue the straight edge of the apron to the red ball under the front point of the collar. Now glue the 10-inch white felt strip along the top of the apron to resemble apron strings. Be sure not to catch any part of the collar under the strip. Overlap the two ends of the white felt strip in back of the red ball to resemble a knot in the apron strings.

Follow the mitten instructions for Santa Claus and glue the mittens on either side of the body on the apron edge, but not on the collar. Glue the pocket on the right side of the apron, and glue the white felt bow at the front point of the collar. Assemble the feet as you did for Santa Claus and glue them to the bottom of the red ball.

Using glitter and glue, make a hairline following the Santa Claus instructions.

Using the red thread and needle, make gathering stitches around the edge of the red felt circle. Pull the stitches and gather the circle so that it fits onto the pink ball like a bonnet. Glue the edge of the bonnet to the head and secure with straight pins while the glue dries. Now glue the 7-inch white felt strip around the edge of the bonnet for a band.

Glue the small white felt dots in position for Mrs. Claus' eyebrows, and then glue the wiggle eyes in position to cover one-half of the white dots. Glue the pink felt dot in place for the nose, and position the red dot for her mouth. Allow the glue to dry.

To make Mrs. Claus' glasses, follow the pattern I outline with the #28 wire. Fit the glasses on her head and glue in place.

Put a dab of glue on the end of the chenille stem, and push it into the hole in the red ball. Thread the needle with the gold cord and make a stitch in the top of Mrs. Claus' hat. Tie the ends together for a hanger.

Santa's Helper

(SEE COLOR INSERT)

Materials

76

Here are the materials and patterns needed for this project.

5″ × 6″ red felt; cut one M, two G, and one ¼″ dot	2″ pink satin ball
2″ x 3″ pink felt; cut two E and one ¼″ dot	2½″ white satin ball
1½″ x 4½″ white felt; cut one C and one N	16″ small gold rickrack
½″ x ½″ black felt; cut two ¼″ dots	8″ gold cord
3″ x 3″ poster board; cut one G	Two 7mm wiggle eyes
	White chenille stem
	Silver glitter
	White glue

Glue the small gold rickrack along the outside edges of the tunic, extending halfway beyond the edge of the felt. Remove the hanger from the white satin ball, and center the opening in the tunic over this hole in the ball. Lay the tunic with the rickrack on the inside, thus revealing a border of one-half the width of the rickrack. Now fasten the tunic to the ball by placing the glue under the felt at the top and under the four corners.

Next glue the collar to the white ball. Position the collar by centering its opening on the hole in the ball. Glue the small black felt dots on the front of the tunic for buttons. Glue the mittens on either side of the ball with the fingers on the tunic. Glue poster board foot between the red felt feet and glue them to the bottom of the white ball.

Using the stem on the pink satin ball as the neck, glue and sprinkle glitter around the top and sides to resemble the outline of hair. Glue the red felt dot in position for a mouth. Now glue the white felt moustache above the mouth. Glue the pink felt dot over the moustache for a nose. Glue the wiggle eyes in position.

Put glue on the stem of the pink ball and push the stem into the hole in the white ball. Put glue on the point of the hook you removed from the white ball and push the hook into the top of the head. Pass the gold cord through the hook and tie the ends of the cord for a hanger.

Angel

(SEE COLOR INSERT)

Materials

Here are the materials and patterns needed for this project.

5" x 10" white felt;
    cut two G, two E, one D
    and 5" diameter circle
¼" x ¼" pink felt; cut one dot
¼" x ¼" red felt; cut one dot
3" x 3" poster board; cut one G
2" pink satin ball
2½" gold satin ball

2" white chenille stem
16" gold braid
40" single loop gold trim
White glitter
Gold glitter
Two 7mm wiggle eyes
White glue

Glue the gold braid around the edge of the circle and cut off any excess braid. Remove the hook from the gold satin ball and line up the hole in the circle with the hole in the gold ball. Glue the circle at the top and at four points around the skirt to form folds. Using 4 inches of the loop trim, make a V-shaped neckline on the front of the skirt. Put a thin line of glue on the cuffs of the mittens and sprinkle with gold glitter. Glue the mittens on the front of the skirt on either side of the V neckline. Glue the felt feet on either side of the poster board feet. Put a dab of glue on the toes of the feet and sprinkle with gold glitter. Glue the feet to the bottom of the gold satin ball.

Using the chenille stem as the neck, spread glue and glitter on the top and sides of the pink ball to resemble hair.

Glue the red dot in position for a mouth and glue the pink dot above that for a nose. Then, glue the eyes in position. Cut off 6¾ inches of loop braid and glue this around the head for a halo. Put glue on the end of the chenille stem and push it into the hole in the gold ball.

Glue the loop braid around the edge of the wings on both sides. Glue the wings onto the skirt, using a dab of glue on each wing and in the center.

Using the hook you removed from the gold ball, put glue on the point of the hook and push into the top of the head. Put the gold cord through the hook and tie the ends for hanging.

Elf

(SEE COLOR INSERT)

Materials

78

Here are the materials and patterns needed for this project.

5" x 7" green felt;
cut one A and one P
4" x 7" red felt;
cut two G, one Q,
1" x 5¾" hatband,
and three ¼" dots
½" x 1¾" white felt;
cut ½" x 1½" rectangular
belt and two ¼" dots
1" x 1" gold felt; cut one D
2" x 2" pink felt;
cut two E and one ¼" dot

3" x 3" poster board; cut one G
2" pink satin ball
2½" gold satin ball
½" red fringe ball
8" gold cord
2" white chenille stem
Red glitter
Two 7mm wiggle eyes
White glue
Needle with large eye
Pinking shears

Trim the two straight edges of the tunic with the pinking shears. Then, remove the hook from the gold satin ball, and place the hole in the tunic over the hole in the ball. Glue it at the top and at the pointed edges. Line up the hole in the red collar with the hole in the tunic and glue in place. Glue the white belt in place on one side of the tunic. Then, glue the gold buckle on the center of the belt, and glue the mittens on either side of the belt. Then, glue the two white dots above the belt for buttons.

Glue one pair of red felt feet to either side of the poster board feet, and then glue the feet to the bottom of the gold ball.

Using the chenille stem as the neck on the pink satin ball, brush glue and sprinkle red glitter to resemble hair. While this dries, make the hat.

Place glue on one straight edge of the green felt, and then place the other straight edge onto the glue to form a cone. Trim one long edge of the hatband with pinking shears. Then glue the straight edge around the bottom of the cone with the pointed edge toward the point of the cone.

Put glue around the inside brim of the hat, and place the hat on the pink ball. Glue the eyes in place. Glue the pink dot on the face for the nose; glue on one red dot for a mouth and use the other two red dots as cheeks. Glue the point of the hat to one side, and then glue the fringe ball onto the point of the hat.

Put glue on the end of the chenille stem, and push it into the hole in the gold ball. Thread the needle with the gold cord, and make one stitch through the top of the hat. Tie the loose ends for a hanger.

79

Soldier

(SEE COLOR INSERT)

Materials

Here are the materials and patterns needed for this project.

7" x 7" white felt;	Small piece black felt;
cut two E, one G, one R, one S,	cut two ¼" dots
one 2¼" circle for hat top,	11" x ⅛" gold trim
and two ¼" dots	10" x ¼" gold braid
4" x 7" poster board;	2" pink satin ball
cut one G, one S, and one	2½" gold satin ball
2¼" circle for hat top	Two 7 mm wiggle eyes
Small piece red felt;	8" gold cord
cut one ¼" dot	2 gold sequin stars
Small piece pink felt;	Gold glitter
cut one ¼" dot	White glue

Glue the gold braid around all six edges of the jacket. Glue 2 inches of the gold trim from the hole in the jacket to one of the shorter edges; this is the front of the jacket. Remove the hook from the gold satin ball. Place the hole in the jacket over the hole in the gold ball, and glue down the jacket at the top and along both short ends. Glue the two stars on the right front of the jacket. Glue ¾ inch of the gold trim on either shoulder to resemble epaulets.

Place glue and sprinkle glitter on the wrist of each mitten. Then, glue the mittens on either side of the jacket front. Glue one pair of feet on either side of the poster feet, and glue the feet to the bottom of the gold ball.

Glue the white felt hat onto the poster board hat. Place glue and sprinkle glitter along the long straight edge of the hat and around the bill of the hat. Then, glue the gold trim along the other long straight edge, making a straight line of trim above the bill in order to separate the bill from the rest of the hat. When this dries, place glue along one of the short sides of the hat and roll this into a tube. Glue the hat top onto the poster board hat top. Then, place a thin line of glue around the top of the tube and place the hat top onto the glue.

Using the chenille stem as the neck, spread glue and sprinkle glitter around the top and sides of the pink ball to resemble hair. When this dries, place glue around the inside brim of the hat and place it on the head. Glue the white dots on the face for eyebrows and glue the black dots half on the white dots. Glue the wiggle eyes onto the black dots. Glue the pink dot in position for the nose and position the red dot for a mouth.

Put glue on the end of the chenille stem and push it into the hole in the gold satin ball. Put glue on the point of the hook you pulled from the gold satin ball and push it into the center of the hat top. Then put the gold cord through the hook and tie the ends for a hanger.

Sailor

(SEE COLOR INSERT)

Materials

Here are the materials and patterns needed for this project.

12" × 15" white felt; cut two E, two G, one T, two ¼" dots, and two 2½" circles for hat	2" pink satin ball 2½" blue satin ball 14" single loop gold braid
½" × ½" red felt; cut one ¼"dot	26" flat gold braid 8" gold cord
½" × ½" pink felt; cut one ¼" dot	White glitter Gold glitter
½" × 1" blue felt; cut two ¼" dots	Small red stars Two 7 mm wiggle eyes
3" × 7" poster board; cut one G and a 2½" circle for hat	White glue

Remove the plastic hook from the blue ball. Glue the poster board between the hat pieces. Trim if necessary. Glue the flat braid around the edge of the hat, thus covering the poster board. Glue red stars on top of the hat. With a sharp point, make a small hole in the center of the hat. Put the plastic hook into his hole.

Using the chenille stem as the neck, brush glue and sprinkle glitter around the top and sides of the pink ball for hair. Let dry. Dip chenille stem into glue and place in top of blue ball, joining head to body.

Glue the flat braid around the edge of the collar and the neck area. Then glue the looped braid around the outside edges, but not the neckline. Glue the red stars on the collar. Fit the collar around the neck and adhere to body with glue at front points and at back of neck.

Spread glue and sprinkle gold glitter on cuff edge of hands and glue at sides of body. Attach the hat to the head by pushing the point of plastic hook into hole at top of pink ball.

Glue the white circles in eye position. Then glue blue circles over the white. Glue the wiggle eyes over the blue circles. Now glue the pink circle for a nose and the red circle for the mouth.

Glue a felt piece to either side of the poster board feet. Let dry. Spread glue across toes of the feet and sprinkle with gold glitter. Glue the feet to bottom of blue ball.

Place gold cord through the plastic loop and knot for a hanging loop.

Snowman

(SEE COLOR INSERT)

Materials

Here are the materials and patterns needed for this project.

5″ × 12″ black felt; cut one U, two V, two E, two G, and four ⅛″ dots

¾″ × 7″ red felt; cut two ½″ × 1″ fringe pieces and three ⅛″ dots

½″ × 7″ green felt scarf

½″ × ½″ white felt; cut two ¼″ dots

5″ × 7″ poster board; cut one G, one U, and one V

2″ white satin ball

2½″ white satin ball

Two ½″ red fringe balls

8″ gold cord

Small plastic corn on pick

White glue

Needle with large eye

Also, cut out the following dimensional strip pieces.

¼″ × 4½″ red felt, for hat trim

1½″ × 4¾″ black felt, for hat crown

1½″ × 4¾″ poster board, for hat crown

Glue the felt hat pieces to the poster board; the poster board hat brim will have felt glued on both sides. Form the crown of the hat by gluing along one narrow edge and rolling on a table to form a tube, slightly overlapping to fit dotted line on hat brim. Put a small amount of glue along the top of the tube and place on the hat brim. Then put glue on the other end of the tube and place small felt circle here. Trim excess felt if necessary. Glue the strips of red felt along the brim of the hat.

Dip one end of the chenille stem into glue and stick halfway into the hole in the large white ball. Brush glue onto chenille sticking out and push into a small ball to form the head. Let dry.

Make fringe, cutting slits ¾ inch deep and ⅛ inch apart. Glue the red fringe to each end of the green felt strips to form a scarf. Wrap scarf around the snowman's neck and glue where it overlaps to hold in place.

Glue the two white dots for eyes. Then glue two small black dots over these to complete the eyes. Glue three black dots down center front of the large ball for the buttons. Adhere the red felt circle for nose. Glue hands to either side of buttons. Glue the hat to the top of the head and the red ball fringe to each side as earmuffs.

Cut the small plastic corn in half. With a sharp point, poke a hole in side of one piece of the corn. Stick a small piece of the pick in the hole. With the sharp point, make a small hole under the nose. Glue the pipe stem into the hole.

Glue one black felt foot to either side of the poster board feet. Let dry. Now glue feet to bottom of the large ball.

Use the needle threaded with the thin gold cord and attach hanging cord to the top of the hat.

Mittens for Your Door

Satin People Ornaments: l. to r. Santa Claus, Mrs. Claus, Santa's Helper, Soldier, Sailor, Snowman, Angel, Elf

Hallway Holly

Millie's Creation

Mom's Santa

Yarn Wreath

Designer Set, Wreath Place Mat and Napkin Ring, Jolly Santa

White Branch a'Hanging

Panoramic Ball with Music Box

Arlene's Golden Tree

More Bazaar Quickies: front l. to r. Whitey Mouse, White Squirrel;
back l. to r. Creche Under Glass, Christmas Pin Cushion

Matilda, Velvet Evergreen, Snow Fun, Della Robbia Tree

Stockings & Tree Skirts

Chapter

6

Millie's Creation
(SEE COLOR INSERT)

Materials

45" × 45" white short nap
fake fur

18" × 24" each of blue, red,
and green felt

12" × 18" each of brown and
yellow felt

9" × 12" each of white and
pink felt

5" × 5" each of gold, black,
and flesh colored felt

1 package red sequins

White glue

Pinking shears

Lay the fake fur material on a flat work surface, with the reverse side up. Mark a 36-inch diameter circle in the center of the material. Now, using a 7-inch diameter salad plate, or a circle template, use one-half of the plate to mark a scalloped edge around the 36-inch circle. Follow the scallop outline while cutting out the material with pinking shears. Cut a 3-inch diameter hole at the center of the circle. Cut a slit in the material from a point between two scallops to the hole in the center.

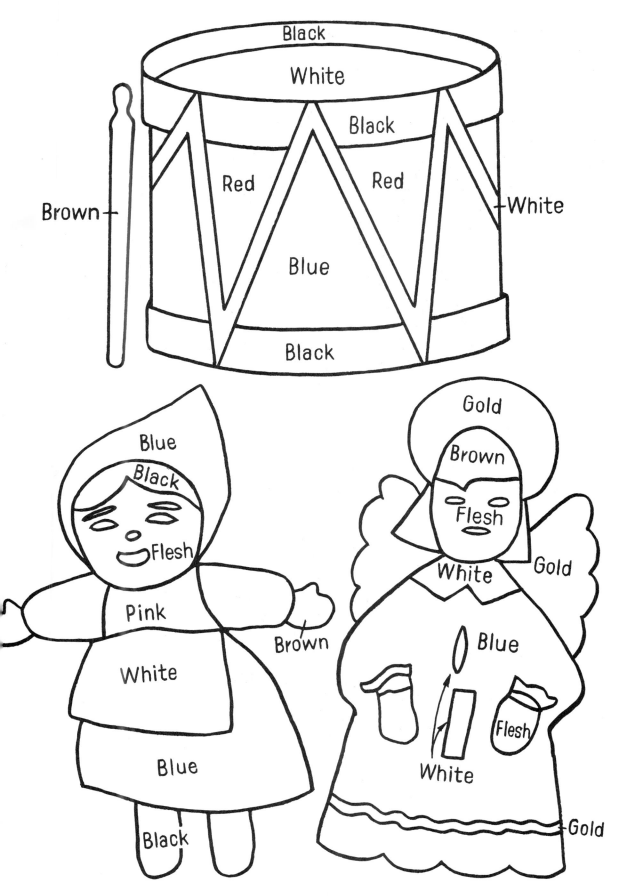

Fig. 6-1 Dutch girl, angel, and drum patterns. These patterns are actual size.

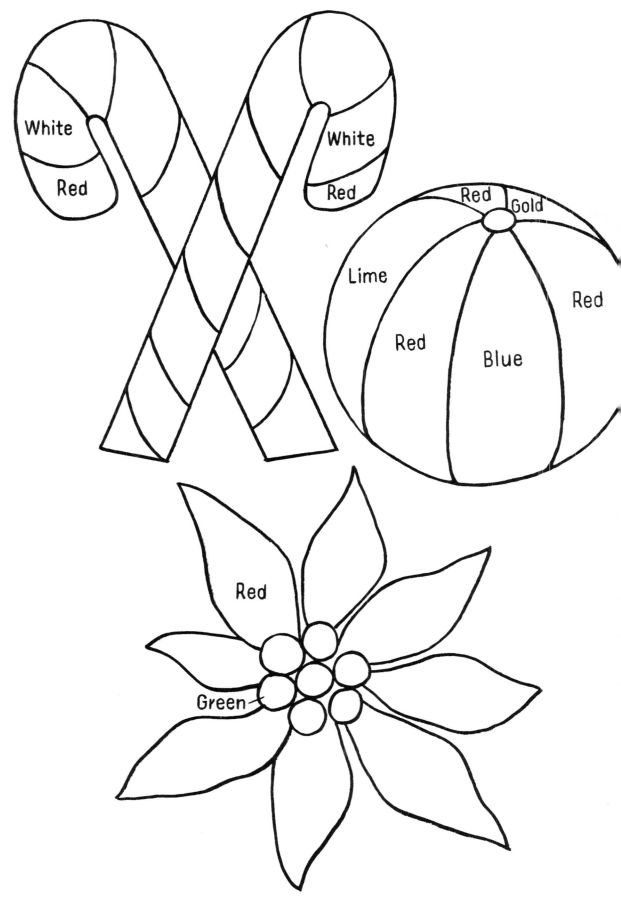

Fig. 6-2 Candy cane, poinsettia, and ball patterns. These patterns are actual size

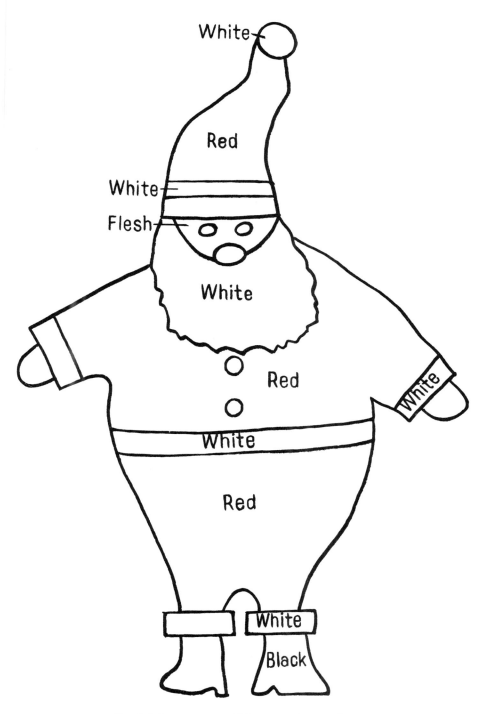

White

Red

White

Flesh

White

Red

White

Black

Red

White

White

Fig. 6-3 Santa pattern. This pattern is actual size.

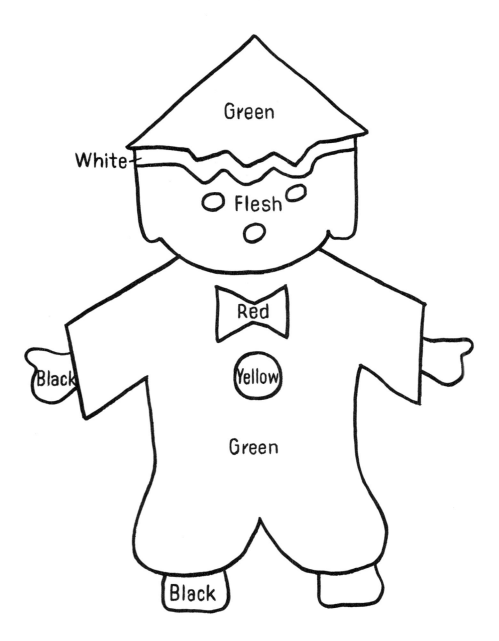

Fig. 6-4 Clown, holly, and tree patterns. These patterns are actual size.

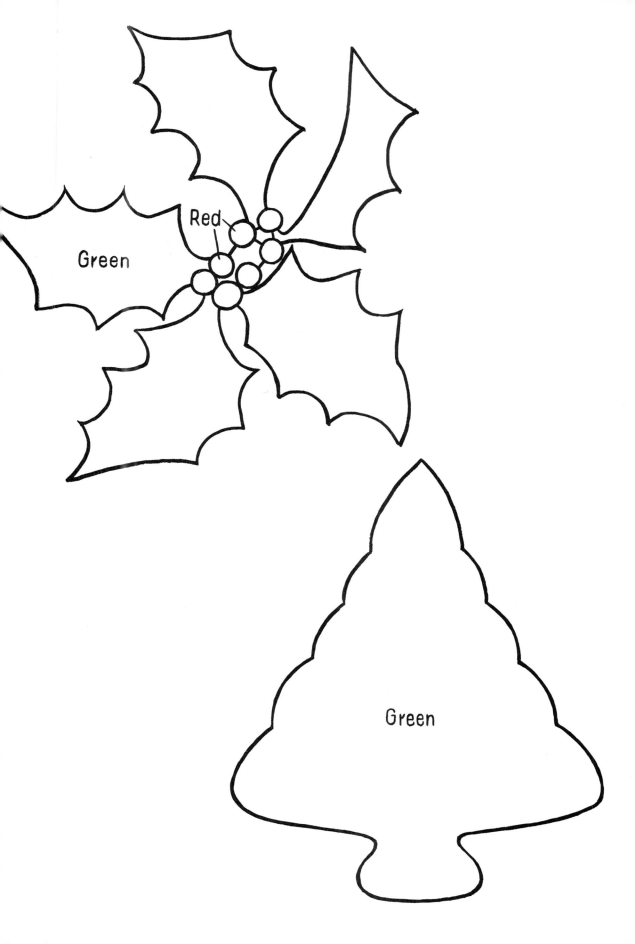

Green

Red

Green

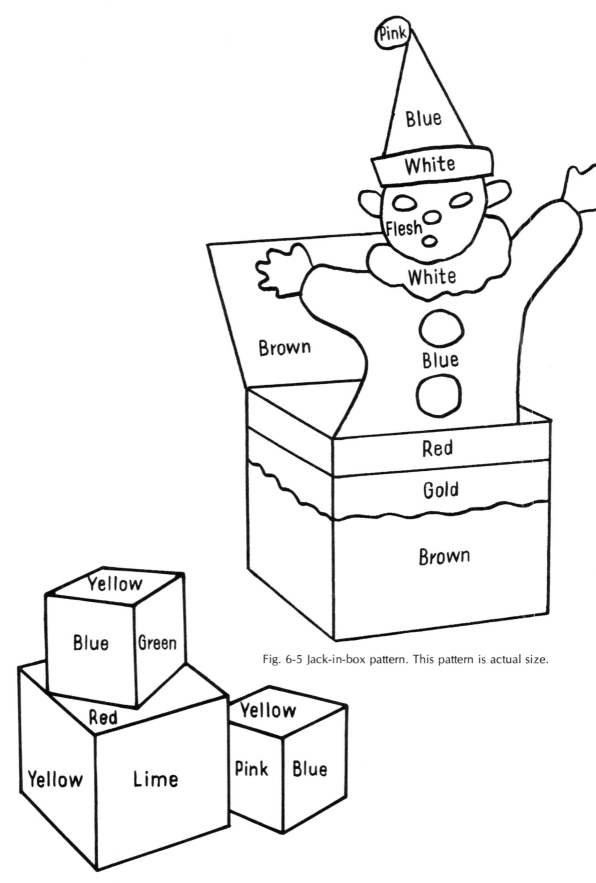

Fig. 6-5 Jack-in-box pattern. This pattern is actual size.

Fig. 6-6 Blocks pattern. This pattern is actual size.

Fig. 6-7 Snowman pattern. This pattern is actual size.

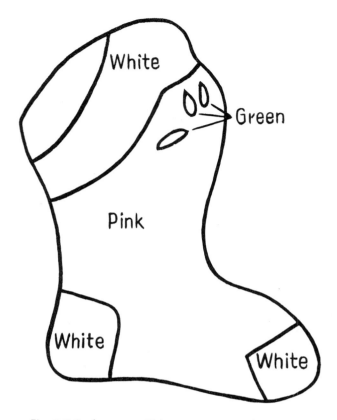

Fig. 6-8 Sock pattern. This pattern is actual size.

Following the patterns in Figs. 6-1 to 6-9, cut the base outline for each decoration from the following colors of felt.

Blue: angel, dutch girl, drum
Red: poinsettia, ball, Santa, candy
    cane
Green: clown, holly, tree

Brown: jack-in-box, Rudolf
Yellow: bell, blocks
White: snowman
Pink: sock

Patterns for Rudolf and the bell are shown below in the directions for the matching stockings.

Also, following the patterns cut out the detail pieces of each decoration from the color of felt as marked on the pattern. Glue each piece of detail in place. Set aside to dry. The tree is completed by gluing sequins on the felt to resemble tree ornaments. As each decoration is completed and dried, spread glue on its back and position it in a scalloped segment of the skirt.

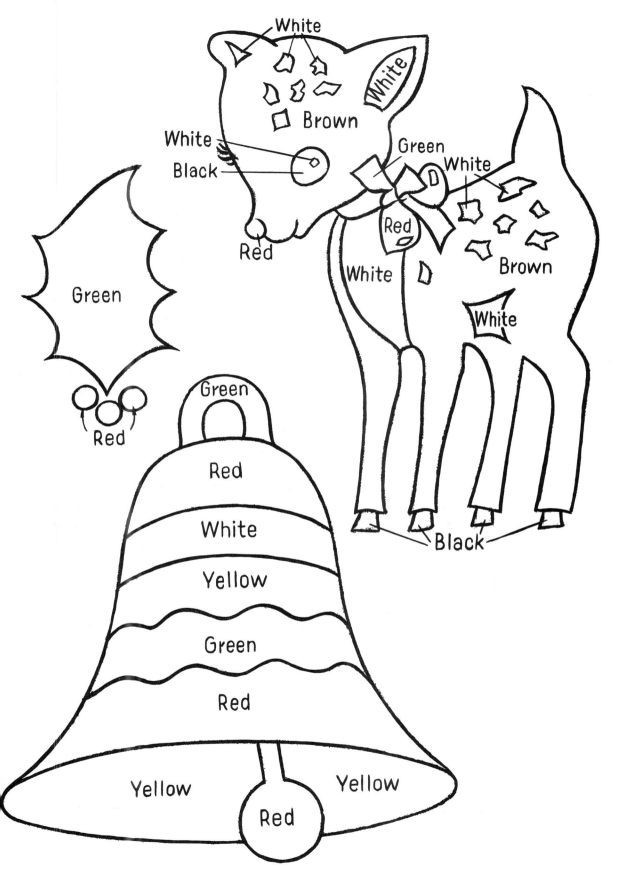

Fig. 6-9 Bell, deer, and holly patterns. These patterns are actual size.

These matching stockings are fun to make and are great bazaar items. Fake fur is available at your local craft shop and many department stores.

Materials

½ yd of 54" wide fake fur
6" × 6" green felt
6" × 6" brown felt
6" × 6" yellow felt
3" × 5" red felt

3" × 3" white felt
1" × 1" black felt
White glue
Pinking shears

Following the patterns in Fig. 6-9, cut the decorations for the stockings from designated colors of felt. Then, to prevent raveling, use the pinking shears to cut two fake fur stockings (Fig. 6-10). Make sure to cut through a double thickness in order to get a front and back for each. With wrong sides together, glue just the edges of the stockings. Let them dry.

For the first stocking, glue the white spots and ears onto Rudolf. Glue the green bow and red bells around his neck. Glue on his eyes and hoofs and don't forget that red nose. Spread glue evenly on the back of Rudolf and place him on the stocking just above the ankle.

Glue three holly leaves and three holly berries at the top of the stocking. Also, glue two holly leaves and three berries at the toe.

For the second stocking, make the whole bell shape from yellow felt—this will be the base for the other stripes on the bell. Assemble it according to the colors shown. Spread glue evenly on the back of the bell and place it about 3 inches above the ankle. Glue three holly berries and three holly leaves at the top of the stocking. At the toe, glue two holly leaves and three berries.

There should be enough fake fur left over for creating stockings of your own. Try trimming them with green felt trees, red candy canes, or angels.

Sue's Design

Materials

3 yd of 36" wide red checked material

10 yd of 1" green ball fringe
Thread

For the tree skirt, cut the full length of the material so that it measures 24 inches wide (Fig. 6-11). To sew the fringe onto the

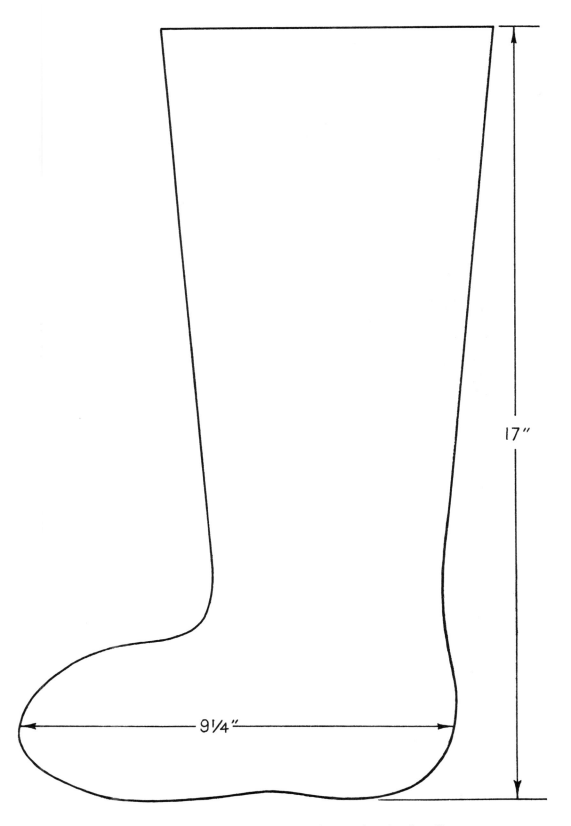

17"

9¼"

Fig. 6-10 Stocking pattern. This pattern has been reduced: ½" = 1"

Fig. 6-11 Sue's Design and Mom's Tree Skirt and Stocking.

material, I suggest using red bobbin thread and green top thread. Turn under ¼ inch along both short sides of material and stitch to prevent raveling.

Cut off 3 yards of the ball fringe and sew the tape of the fringe on the selvage edge of the material with a small zigzag stitch. Turn under the ends of the fringe and stitch them so they do not ravel.

Stitch and make long gatherings the length of the material 8 inches from the selvage, 16 inches from the selvage, and along the long cut edge of the material. Pull the first row of stitching, which is 8 inches from the selvage, so that it measures 2½ yards. Cut off 2½ yards of ball fringe and zigzag stitch the tape at the fringe over the gathering stitches. Be sure to have the balls hanging toward the selvage and turn under the ends of the fringe to prevent raveling.

Pull the next row of stitching so that it measures 1⅓ yards. Cut off 1⅓ yards of ball fringe and zigzag stitch the tape of fringe over the gathering stitches. Pull the last row of stitching so that it measures 11 inches and then stitch 11 inches of fringe over the gathering stitches.

Using the pattern in Fig. 6-10, cut a stocking from a double thickness of the red checked material. Turn under ¼ inch along the top of both pieces of the stockings and stitch to prevent raveling. Allowing for ½-inch seam, stitch the right sides of the two stocking pieces together. Do not stitch across the top. Turn the stocking to the right side and press with a steam iron.

Cut off 54 inches of ball fringe to go around the stocking. Starting on one side, zigzag stitch the tape of the fringe on the edge of the stocking. Hand stitch the fringe across the top of the stocking, being sure to leave the stocking open.

Mom's Tree Skirt and Stocking

Materials

36" × 45" red felt	9 assorted Christmas cards
7 yd of ¾" white and gold lace	Christmas gift tag
½ yd white nylon net	Needle and white thread
1 package snow flake sequins	White glue
Assortment of sequins	

Cut a 36-inch diameter circle from the red felt for the tree skirt. Fold the circle in quarters and mark the point; this is the center. Cut a 2-inch diameter circle at the center. Cut a slit from the outside edge directly to the center circle. Cut two stockings from the red felt, following the pattern outline in Fig. 6-10. Press the felt pieces with a steam iron to remove all the wrinkles.

Lay one red felt stocking piece on a flat surface, with the toe pointed to the right (Fig. 6-11). Glue white and gold lace all around the edge, except at the top of the stocking (Fig. 6-11). Position the lace so that it extends beyond the edges of the felt. Spread more glue on the edge of the stocking. Now place the second stocking piece over the first and press the edges firmly. Keep the top of the stocking open for stuffing on Christmas Eve. Set aside to dry.

Glue white and gold lace around the outside edge of the skirt. Allow the glue to dry.

Cut nylon net wide enough to cover each of the Christmas cards and the gift tag and long enough to wrap around the cards and tag with the ends meeting in back. Wrap each card and the tag, and sew the seam with a needle and thread.

Using needle, thread and an assortment of sequins, decorate the cards. For instance, if one of your cards has a wreath on it with fruit decorations, sew a large gold snowflake sequin topped by a small red or green sequin over one of the pears. On top of an apple, sew a blue spoke sequin topped by a small red sequin. Fill in the spaces with other sequins.

Try to use an assortment of Christmas cards with various designs. Do your own thing! Decorate the candles, Santa, and baubles to your heart's content.

When you have all the sequins sewn on your cards, glue white and gold lace around the edges of all the cards and the gift tag too.

Use a long card for the top of the stocking. Spread glue on the back of the card and lay it horizontally at the top and press firmly. This makes a nice cuff. Place another card at the center of the stocking and glue in place. Glue the gift tag at the toe of the stocking. Scatter white snowflake sequins over the stocking and secure with glue.

Arrange the seven other cards around the tree skirt to suit your fancy. Spread glue on the back of the cards and press in place. Fill in the spaces by gluing white snowflake sequins here and there.

Now you're ready to put the skirt under the tree and hang the stocking on the mantle.

Hobby Stocking

Make a personalized Christmas stocking for the guitar player in your family. Our twin daughters both play the guitar and they love this creation (Fig. 6-12).

Materials

20" × 20" yellow felt; cut two stockings (Fig. 6-10)	6" × 22" poster board; cut guitar handle (Fig. 6-13)
6" × 10" black felt; cut five musical notes (Fig. 6-13)	20" red yarn
	Three ¼" yellow wooden beads
5" × 17" brown felt; cut guitar handle (Fig. 6-13)	30" yellow cord
	White glue

Also, cut out the following dimensional pieces.

Five ⅜" × 6⅝" black felt strips	¾" × 10" poster board strip
¾" × 16½" brown felt strip	¾" × 11½" poster board strip

Spread glue in ½-inch seam around the edge of one of the yellow felt stockings. Lay the other stocking onto the first and press the glued seam together. Set aside to dry.

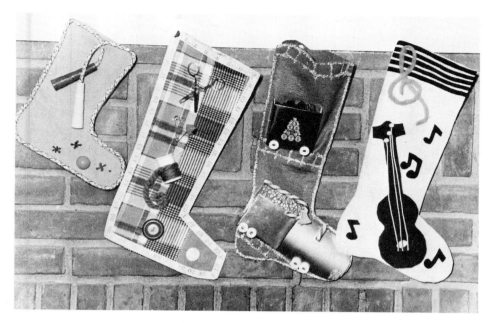

Fig. 6-12 Girl's, Sewing, Choo-Choo, and Hobby Stockings.

With each of the two poster board strips, make a circular piece which resembles a donut. Overlap the ends ½ inch and glue to hold. Place the circular pieces side by side with the seams touching. Glue these two together to form a figure eight. Allow the glue to dry.

Trace the figure eight onto poster board and cut it out. Also, cut a matching figure eight out of brown felt. Cut the felt just slightly larger than the poster board. Glue the felt onto the poster board, form the felt down over the edges of the poster board. Trim away the excess. In the center of the larger half of the figure eight, cut out a one-inch diameter hole. This will resemble the sound box.

Starting at the top of the smaller of the two circles, glue the brown felt strip around the outside of the figure. Make a slight indentation on both sides where the circles are glued together. These indentations should match the figure eight you have traced. Now glue the figure eight onto the two circles.

Next, glue the brown felt guitar handle onto the poster board guitar handle. Glue the handle onto the smaller part of the figure eight, about ¼ inch in from the edge. Allow to dry. Position the guitar on the yellow stocking and glue in place.

Cut the yellow cord into three lengths—9 inches, 9½ inches, and 10 inches. These are the strings for the guitar. Glue one end of each

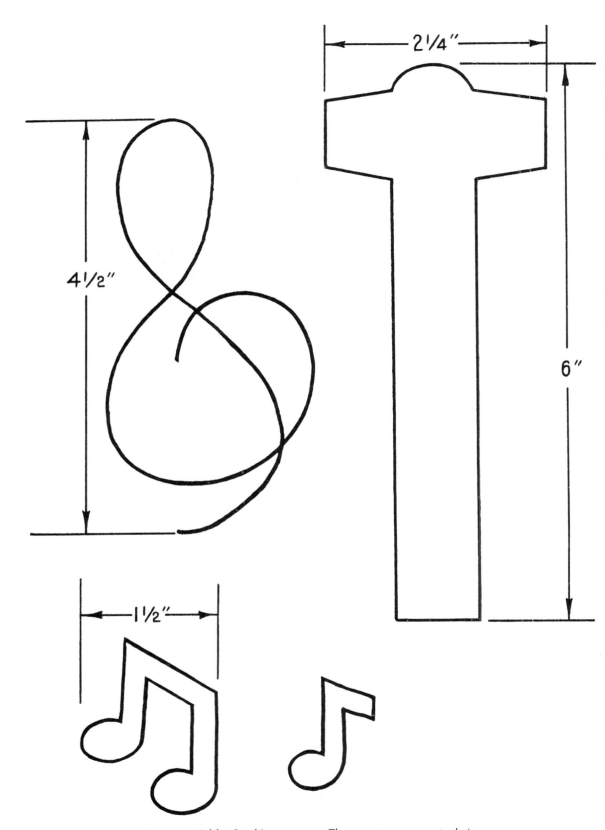

Fig. 6-13 Hobby Stocking patterns. These patterns are actual size.

string ⅛ inch below the hole in the base of the guitar. Then glue each of the other ends at the cross bar in the handle. Make the cords as taut as possible. Now glue one yellow bead on the handle end of each string.

Glue the black felt strips at the top of the stocking, with a ¼-inch space between each strip. This will resemble a musical scale. Glue the red yarn on the left of the scale in the shape of a treble clef.

Glue three black felt musical notes on the scale; glue one note on the heel and the other on the toe.

Choo-Choo Stocking

The train is made from last year's Christmas cards (Fig. 6-12). I used the back page of three foil cards to construct the engine and the coal car. The tree on the coal car, the stained glass window, and the train's bell were also cut from Christmas cards. The candy wheels and the candy cane roof are glued to the stocking, but the coal car is filled with licorice candy.

Materials

20″ × 20″ green felt	Small bell card
3½″ × 3½″ × 1″ cardboard	6 small candy circles
gift box	Wrapped candy cane
5½″ × 5½″ blue foil	Package of bite-size licorice
6½″ × 9½″ gold foil	Silver glitter
1½″ × 4″ stained glass card	White glue
Small gold tree card	

Following the pattern in Fig. 6-10, cut a stocking from a double thickness of green felt. Making a ½-inch seam except at the top, glue the two pieces of the stocking together. Place a line of glue around all the edges of the stocking and then sprinkle with glitter. Place glue and glitter in the shape of a train track across the heel of the stocking, halfway up the stocking, and across the top of the stocking. While this dries, build the train engine and coal car.

Cut a 4½-inch square from the gold foil. Cover the top of the cardboard box with this piece of foil and glue in place. Glue the stained glass card along one edge of the box so that half of the card extends past the edge of the box. Break off 1½ inches of the candy cane. Then, glue the candy cane along the top of the stained glass card with the hook of the cane facing downward. Then, glue the bell cut from a card onto the hook of the candy cane. Glue two candy circles on the bottom of the box at the opposite corner from the bell.

Cut a 4-inch by 5½-inch rectangle from the gold foil and round off the corners on one of the 4-inch sides. Place the short straight edge to the left, make lines of glue and sprinkle glitter on the lower curve to resemble a cowcatcher.

Glue the gold box on top of the tracks that go across the heel. Roll the rectangle to give it a curve so that when you glue it to the stocking, it stands out slightly. Glue the rectangle next to the box, matching the bottom edges. Glue two candy circles in the center of the bottom edge of the rectangle. Then, glue the 1½-inch length of candy cane in the center top edge of the rectangle.

Cut off one side of the bottom of the box. This is the top where the coal is placed. Then, cover the box with the blue foil. Glue the gold tree onto the center of the blue foil. Glue two candy circles on the bottom corners of the box. Glue the blue box above the tracks in the middle of the stocking.

When all the glue dries, hang the train and fill the coal car with licorice.

Girl's Stocking

Materials

11" × 18" orange felt	Ball and 3 jacks
Jump rope	

For this stocking, you will use the same pattern as for the others, except the leg will be 6 inches shorter. Be sure to cut the stocking from a double thickness of orange felt. Make a ½-inch seam, glue the two pieces of the stocking together. Be sure to leave the top of the stocking open so Santa will be able to stuff it with goodies.

You will be using 45 inches of jump rope so if your rope is longer, cut off the extra length and reassemble the handle onto the rope (Fig. 6-12). Glue the rope around the edge of the stocking. Let about 4 inches of the ends hang into the center of the stocking. Glue the handles in place.

Glue the jacks and the ball at the toe of the stocking. Let the glue dry.

Sewing Stocking

In our stocking, we used colors that would match the material (Fig. 6-12). You can match your buttons and yarn with the patchwork material that you obtain.

Materials

20″ × 20″ patchwork material	1″ button
20″ yarn	Empty foam spool
Tape measure	Large safety pin
Snub nose scissors	Small pin cushion
1¾″ button	White glue
	Serrated edge knife

Using the pattern in Fig. 6-10, cut a stocking from a double thickness of the patchwork material. Making a ½-inch seam, glue the wrong sides of the stocking together, except at the top. Leave the top of the stocking open so Santa can stuff it with sewing accessories for the seamstress.

Glue the tape measure around all edges of the stocking, forming corners as previously described wherever the stocking curves. Cut off any of the excess tape measure.

Cut the spool in half lengthwise with a serrated edge knife. Wrap the yarn around the spool four times and glue in place. Do not cut off the excess yarn.

Glue the scissors at the center top of the stocking in an open position. Open the safety pin and put glue on the point of the pin. Push the pin into the pin cushion. Glue the pin and pin cushion about 1½ inches below the scissors. Glue the spool wrapped with yarn about 1½ inches below the pin cushion. Glue the excess yarn below the spool in a curlicue shape. Glue the larger button below the spool and a little to the right. Glue the smaller button at the toe of the stocking.

Bazaar
Quickies

Chapter 7

Christmas Birdhouse

The base for the birdhouse was cut from a large pine cone we collected on a vacation trip through Georgia. My father has built dozens of these miniature birdhouses using wood scraps, yardsticks, and medicine applicator sticks (Fig. 7-6).

Materials

2" × 2" red felt
1" × 1" green felt
6" of ³/₃₂" dowel, or
    applicator stick
2" of ⁵/₃₂" × 1¼" wood
    strip, or yardstick
⅞" × ¾" × ¾" block
    of wood
Two 1" white ball fringe
Two 10mm wiggle eyes

Large pine cone
Dried materials: small cones,
    stems
Sphagnum moss
Floral clay
White glue
Small plastic bird
Red paint
White paint

106

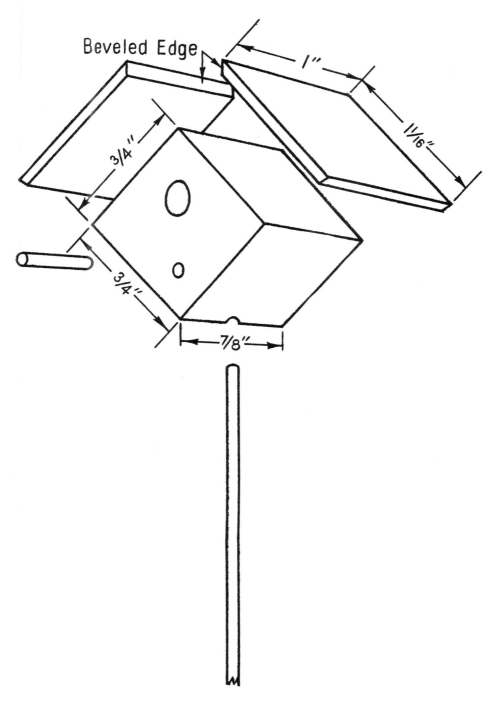

Fig. 7-1 Christmas Birdhouse sketch.

First assemble the birdhouse (Fig. 7-1). Cut roof pieces from the $5/32$-inch material. Instead of a yardstick, these pieces can be cut from regular wood stock or balsa wood. Each roof piece is to be 1 by $1^1/_{16}$ inches long. Bevel one of the one inch sides to a 45° angle on each piece. Set aside.

Form the house piece into a ¾ by ¾ × ⅞-inch block. On one end of the block, drill a $3/_{16}$-inch hole, ¼-inch deep, to resemble a birdhouse entrance. Below the entrance, drill a $3/_{32}$-inch hole for mounting the perch. Glue the roof pieces onto the house, centering the pieces so that equal amounts overhang at the front and back. Set aside.

After the glue for the roof pieces has dried, drill a $3/_{32}$-inch hole, ¼-inch deep, at the center of the bottom edge of the house for inserting the mounting pole. Cut a ½-inch long piece off of the $3/_{32}$-inch dowel for the perch. Place a dab of glue on one end of the perch and push it into the $3/_{32}$-inch hole on the front of the birdhouse. Place another dab of glue on one end of the 5½-inch piece of dowel and push it into the bottom $3/_{32}$-inch hole. Allow the glue to dry. Paint and trim the birdhouse. After the paint is dry, glue the bird onto the top of the house.

The birdhouse base is cut from the stem end of a large pine cone. A bandsaw or fine-toothed hand saw is best for cutting pine cones. The birdhouse is attached to the pine cone base with floral clay. Put a small amount of floral clay around the bottom end of the birdhouse pole. Place the pole on top of the pine cone and press the floral clay firmly around the pole and onto the pine cone base.

Spread white glue over the floral clay and around the top of the base. Arrange sphagnum moss on the glue to partially cover the top of the base. Arrange the dried materials, miniature pine cones, and stems over the base, using white glue to secure them.

The Christmas cat is created from ball fringe, wiggle eyes, and felt. Start by gluing the two white ball fringe pieces together. Cut ears, nose, tail, and feet from red felt. Cut holly leaves from green felt. Glue all the felt pieces in correct position on the ball fringe. Glue two wiggle eyes on the face to complete the cat.

Set the cat on the base and your Christmas birdhouse is ready for display.

Skier

(SEE FRONT COVER)

It is fun to make animals and people from ball fringe. Ball fringe comes in many sizes and colors, some even come with faces on them. I will give you a few ideas and then you can try to create your own.

Materials

1" red fringe ball	White chenille stem
1" face fringe ball	2 round toothpicks
1½" × 3" gold paper	White glue
2 green snowflake sequins	

Glue the face fringe ball on top of the red fringe ball. Cut one 3-inch length of chenille stem and curl the two ends slightly to form hands. Glue the center of the stem at the back of the skier where the two balls are joined.

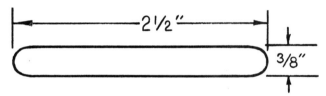

Fig. 7-2 Ski pattern. This pattern is actual size.

Using the pattern in Fig. 7-2, cut two skis from the gold paper. Glue them to the bottom of the red fringe ball. Slip a snowflake sequin over the end of each toothpick. Glue the other end into the chenille stem hands.

Like magic, you have a skier ready for the bazaar.

Clown

(SEE FRONT COVER)

Materials

1" × 1" white felt	Two ¾" red, white, and blue
2" × 2" white burlap	fringe balls
Face fringe ball	Red felt dot
Two ½" red fringe balls	

Glue the two red, white, and blue fringe balls together. Glue the two red fringe balls together. Then, glue the red balls on top of the other two balls. Glue the face fringe ball centered atop the red fringe balls.

Cut a circle of white burlap the size of a nickel. For the crown of the hat, you use such a small piece of burlap that it is not necessary to use a pattern. Cut a small piece, roll easily into a cone shape, and glue the seam. Attach the open end of the cone to the burlap circle with glue. Now, glue the hat to the head.

Cut small circles from white felt for two hands, two feet, and two buttons. Glue them in the proper places. Glue the red dot to the top of the clown's hat.

Jumpin' Jack
(SEE FRONT COVER)

Materials

Face fringe ball	9" elastic cord
Six ¾" red, white, and blue fringe balls	White glue
	Large eye needle

Glue three fringe balls together in a straight line. Glue the face fringe ball on top of the center ball. Below the center ball fringe, glue one red, white, and blue fringe ball for the bottom of his body. To that, glue the other two ball fringes on a diagonal for Jack's legs.

Sew the cord through the center top of the face fringe ball. Tie the ends together and hang Jumpin' Jack on a tree or use him to trim a package.

Matilda
(SEE COLOR INSERT)

Materials

5" Styrofoam ball	Red chenille bump
6" Styrofoam ball	8mm pink bead
Three 2" Styrofoam balls	3 red 12mm beads
8" × 8" × ½" Styrofoam block	3 corsage pins
2 yd of 1" red and white checked ribbon	3 gold paper medallions
Small holly candle ring	Two 12mm wiggle eyes
2 gold rings	Boxwood green pick
Black chenille stem	8 toothpicks
2 green chenille stems	6" #28 wire
	White glue
	Serrated edge knife

Cut a piece of ribbon 32 inches long. Spread glue on the ribbon and cover the top side edges of the Styrofoam block, extending the ribbon ½ inch over the edge. Fold the extra ½-inch width of ribbon to the top of the Styrofoam block.

Put glue on two toothpicks and stick them together in the center top of the Styrofoam block. Put glue on the exposed ends of the toothpicks. Secure the 6-inch Styrofoam ball to the base by pushing the center of the ball down firmly over the toothpicks.

Put two toothpicks very close together in the top center of the large ball. Attach the 5-inch ball to the other ball by pushing it down over the toothpicks.

Put one toothpick in two of the 2-inch balls. Place these in position for arms, sticking the toothpicks in the larger ball.

Using a serrated edge knife, cut the other 2-inch ball in half. Put a toothpick in each half of the ball near the cut edge. Keeping the flat side against the base, push each toothpick into the bottom front of the larger ball. These are Matilda's feet.

Glue the wiggle eyes in place; glue a pink bead in position for a nose; shape the red bump chenille for the mouth and glue in place. Cut two 2-inch pieces of black chenille stem; shape them for eyebrows; glue them in place. The two gold rings will serve as earrings, so glue one on each side of the face in position.

Cut a 20-inch length of ribbon to go around the center of the large ball for a belt. For buttons, glue the three gold paper medallions on the front of the largest ball. Push a corsage pin through a large red bead and then put it in the center of the medallion. Repeat for other two buttons.

Arrange the boxwood green pieces around the base. Cut the boxwood green pick into several pieces. Cut the green chenille stem into 2-inch pieces and bend the pieces into U shapes. Secure the greens in place by pushing the U-shaped pieces over the stem and into the Styrofoam base.

Center the small candle ring on top of the head. Use two U-shaped chenille stems to attach the ring to the ball as a hat.

Make a double loop bow from the remaining ribbon, and tie the bow with #28 wire. Use the wire to secure the bow to Matilda's head in the center of the candle ring.

Now Matilda is ready for your table. She makes you want to smile.

Velvet Evergreen

(SEE COLOR INSERT)

112

This is a basic design that lends to a variety of arrangements. It can be used with a collection of evergreens of different sizes or by itself. After you have mastered the method, decorate the tree in different ways.

Materials

6" Styrofoam cone	1" high angel
5 yd moss green velvet tubing	Black plastic top hat
2 yd of 3mm pearls	10 straight pins
Pearl triple crown	White glue

Starting at the point of the cone, glue the velvet tubing one row at a time in a spiral fashion. Pin the tubing at random to prevent slipping. Be careful not to let glue get onto the side of the tubing that shows, because the glue will look messy when it dries. Cover the entire tree.

Glue one end of the strand of pearls on the top of the cone. Place the pearls in the same spiral direction as the tubing and glue at random. There should be about a ¾-inch space between each row of pearls. You will have a small section of the strand left, so cut it off.

For the trunk of the tree, you will use the top hat. Glue the leftover strand of pearls around the brim of the hat. Let it dry and then glue the top of the hat to the bottom center of the tree. Next glue the triple crown on the top of the tree and then glue the angel on top of that.

Dandy Christmas Pandy

(SEE FRONT COVER)

Materials

Two 2" Styrofoam balls	1" x 1" white felt
Sixteen 3" red chenille bumps	3 red flowers
Twenty 3" white chenille bumps	2 toothpicks
1" x 1" red felt	White glue
1" x 1" black felt	

Cut fourteen single white chenille bumps. Put one end of a white bump into the Styrofoam ball at a place we'll call the top; wrap the bump around the Styrofoam and insert the other end into what would be the bottom of the ball. Use all fourteen bumps to completely cover one ball. This will be the head.

Cut six single white chenille bumps and eight single red chenille bumps. For the chest, insert six white bumps on the second Styrofoam ball. Use the eight red bumps to finish covering the ball.

Insert two toothpicks into the head where all the bumps meet. To attach the two balls together, put a dab of glue on the toothpick and push the toothpick into the other ball where the points of the bumps meet.

From the black felt, cut a triangular-shaped nose, two circles ⅜ inch in diameter and two circles with a ⅛-inch diameter. Cut two circles with a ¼-inch diameter from the white felt. Glue the white circles on the large black circles and then glue the small black circles on top of the white ones. Presto—eyes! The face is just above the white chest; glue the nose and eyes in position. Cut a teardrop shaped tongue from the red felt. Glue it just under the nose.

Cut seven single red chenille bumps. For each ear, fold a single red bump in half and twist the cut ends together. Insert in the correct place.

Fold four red bumps in half and put them into the body for arms and legs. Shape the folded end of the arms for paws. Fold one red chenille bump in half and shape it for a tail. Put it at the bottom back of Dandy's body. Push the flowers' stem into the Styrofoam between the ears.

Isn't she a dandy Christmas pandy?

Pine Cone Lassies

(SEE FRONT COVER)

Materials

Two 3" pine cones	White chenille stem
2 hazelnuts	Silicone adhesive
2" x 20" red material	2 toothpicks
12" yellow yarn	Needle and thread

Cook the two hazelnuts for one hour at 200°. This will keep them from spoiling. Using needle nose pliers, break off a few petals on the small end of a cone. Put some silicone adhesive on the round part of the hazelnut and press into the cut part of the cone, keeping flat part of the hazelnut as the face of the figure.

Cut a piece of red material 2 by 9 inches. Pull threads on one long side and one end; keep pulling threads until there's a fringe ½-inch wide.

Thread needle and run a gathering stitch on the unfringed, long side of the material. With a toothpick, spread some silicone adhesive under the third row of petals on the pine cone. With a clean toothpick, poke the center of red material under the petals at the center front of the cone. Continue poking the material under petals, gathering the material on the thread as you go. Make the two ends meet at the back center. Make a few stitches, tacking one piece to the other. This will help hold the skirt until the adhesive dries.

Cut a trianglular piece of red material, 2 inches at the base and 1 inch high to the point. Use silicone adhesive to adhere this under the hazelnut face. This becomes her blouse.

Cut a 6-inch piece of white chenille stem and shape as arms. Bend around the pine cone and secure with silicone adhesive at the center back.

Cut yellow yarn into 6-inch pieces. Tie a knot near each end. Spread adhesive over the top of the hazelnut head and lay the yarn hair in place. Make sure the hair comes down around her face.

Make the second lassie the same way, omitting blouse and arms.

Pine Cone Basket

(SEE FRONT COVER)

Materials

2" wide x 2½" high pine cone	Red chenille stem
1 dozen miniature artificial fruits	Silicone adhesive

Use a pine cone with a flat bottom so the basket will sit straight. Break off the first two rows of petals on the small end of the pine cone; needle nose pliers are great for this job.

Cut wires off the artificial fruit. Put a dab of silicone adhesive on one side of six pieces of fruit. Lay these fruit on the cone where you cut off the petals. Let dry. Now arrange the rest of the fruits and use silicone adhesive to adhere in place.

Cut a 4-inch piece of red chenille stem and shape for the handle. Put silicone adhesive on each end of the handle and stick ends under the fruit. Make several pine cone baskets for that church bazaar.

Mouse-in-a-Walnut

Materials

3″ x 3″ brown, short
    nap fake fur
2″ x 4″ red and white
    gingham material
1″ Styrofoam ball
3 red rocaille beads

6″ gold cord
Half of an English walnut shell
Cotton ball
Needle and brown thread
White glue

Trace the patterns in Fig. 7-3 for the mouse's head and tail onto the wrong side of the fake fur and cut out. Glue the back of the ears to the front of the ears, do not glue the area between the A's. Sew the top of the head together, matching front to back and sewing from A to A. Stuff the head with part of the cotton ball. Now fold and sew between the B's. Sew through mouth area three times, leaving ½ inch thread loops. Cut the loops to resemble whiskers. Glue the rocaille beads onto the face for the eyes and nose. Fold the tail in half lengthwise and glue together.

Shape the Styrofoam ball to fit inside the walnut shell half. Flatten one side of the ball and leave the other side rounded for the mouse's tummy. Place glue on the flat side of the ball and place it inside the shell. Glue the mouse's head to the Styrofoam ball at the flat end of the walnut shell. Glue the tail at the other end.

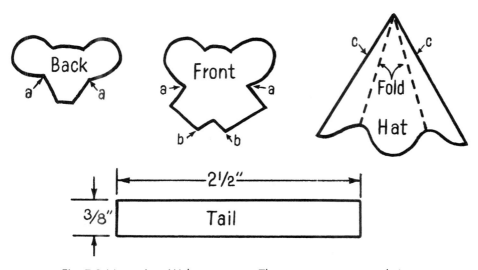

Fig. 7-3 Mouse-in-a-Walnut patterns. These patterns are actual size.

Cut a 2 by 2-inch piece of red and white gingham material. Fringe one end for ¼-inch. Tuck the other end under the mouse's chin and glue in place. Also, glue the sides of the material to the walnut shell. This makes a nice blanket for the mouse.

Cut the hat from the red and white gingham material, following the pattern outline. Fold on the dotted lines and glue C to C. Keeping the bill of the hat to the front, glue the hat on the mouse's head. Glue a tiny piece of cotton to the tip of the hat. Tuck each end of the gold core at the center of the shell under the edge of the blanket. Glue in place.

Your mouse is ready to hang on the tree. Wouldn't a group of these be cute on a wreath?

Matchbox House

(SEE FRONT COVER)

Materials

2 small boxes of matches	2½" x 2½" poster board
3" x 3" green felt	Silver glitter
1" x 3" red felt	White glue
2¼" x 7½" natural colored burlap	Rubber band

Spread glue on the top side of one matchbox. Lay the other matchbox onto the glued surface, keeping the striking surface of both matchboxes adjacent to each other. Wrap a rubber band tightly around the boxes and leave until the glue is dry. The striking surfaces of the matchboxes are to be kept on the bottom of the house.

Spread glue on one side of the burlap. Wrap the burlap onto the sides and top of the matchboxes, being careful to keep the burlap and glue off the bottom, striking surfaces and both ends.

Glue the green felt to the piece of poster board. Fold in half. Put glue along both upper edges of the covered matchboxes. Holding the felt and poster board piece in the shape of a roof, place the poster board onto the glue edges. Hold in place until glue is tacky.

Now spread a small amount of glue along the edges of the felt roof. Sprinkle the silver glitter onto the glue for a snowy effect.

Using the red felt, cut three ½ by 1-inch pieces and four ½ by ½-inch pieces. Take one of the ½ by 1-inch pieces and spread glue on half of its length. Now place a second ½ by 1-inch piece on top of the first. Spread the loose ends and place glue on both. Set this piece with the loose ends over each side of the roof, thus forming the chimney.

Glue the third ½ by 1-inch piece to the center on one side of the box for a door. Now glue a ½ by ½-inch piece on each side of door for windows. Glue the other two ½ by ½-inch pieces on the opposite side for windows also.

Add this to your items for that bazaar.

Nativity

(SEE BACK COVER)

Baskets come in many shapes and sizes and therefore offer you a variety of arrangements. Use your imagination and see what you can make.

Materials

Basket with one flat side	6 small pine cones
Plastic nativity set	White glue
Sphagnum moss	

Using your finger, spread white glue on the roof of the nativity set. Lay small pieces of sphagnum moss into the glue. Let dry. Spread white glue all over the inside of the basket. Place sphagnum moss on the glue. Let dry.

Stand the basket on the flat side. This is the bottom of the arrangement. You may want to glue more moss around the base of the nativity. Glue the small pine cones to the corners of the basket.

Put a lot of white glue on the bottom of the nativity set and position it firmly in the center of the basket at the bottom.

Crocheted Snowman

(SEE FRONT COVER)

Materials

4 oz. skein white knitting worsted	½" × ½" black felt
Crochet hook size 4 or E	Cotton or tissue to stuff head
Two 10mm wiggle eyes	Purchased hat, 3" in diameter
1" × 10" red felt	

The following abbreviations are used in the directions.

ch—chain   sl st—slip stitch   sp—space   dc—double crochet

Chain 8, sl st in 1st st to form circle. Each row begins with 3 ch st. Each row ends with 1 sl st to fasten. Row 1: Into circle make 16 dc. Row 2: To widen this row, make 2 dc in every other space and 1 dc in each sp in between. This will equal 24 dc and make it curve for the top of the head. Row 3: 1 dc in each space equal 24 dc. Rows 4, 5, 6: Repeat row 3, this forms the head. Row 7: 1 dc in next 3 sp, skip 1 sp, and repeat to make a row. Row 8: 1 dc in each sp, this narrow to make the neck. Row 9: To widen for shoulders, 1 dc in next 3 sp, then 2 dc in 4th sp, and repeat to finish row. Rows 10, 11: Repeat row 9. Rows 12, 13, 14: 1 dc in each sp, 40 dc. Row 15: To narrow, make 1 dc in next 4 sp, skip 1 sp, repeat to finish row. This forms the body. Row 16: Repeat row 15.

In row 8, draw piece of yarn through to pull neck up a bit.

Cut the following pieces from the red felt.

⅛" circle for nose	½" x 10" scarf
Mouth	⅛" x 5" hatband

Cut from the black felt:

Two ¼" circles for buttons	Two ⅛" circle for eyes

Finish the snowman by gluing the scarf, hatband, nose, mouth, and eyes in position.

If you want to make the hat yourself, see the directions for the "Snow Fun" hat.

Mom's Santa

(SEE COLOR INSERT)

My mother has been creating Christmas decorations for years. Once again, her talent shines and she presents this Santa to you.

Materials

15" x 18" red felt	1" diameter red ball fringe
5" x 5" red felt	9" lightweight cord
2" x 14" white felt	3" x 5" angel hair
½" x 12" white felt	Two 10mm wiggle eyes
9" x 12" poster board	Diamond dust
2" diameter x 3" long	White glue
Styrofoam dowel	Masking tape
3" Styrofoam ball	Black felt tip pen

Using the pattern outlines in Fig. 7-4 and 7-5, cut out the following items:

Red felt cone, large pattern	White felt snow
Red felt hat, small pattern	Poster board cone, large pattern
Red felt mouth	

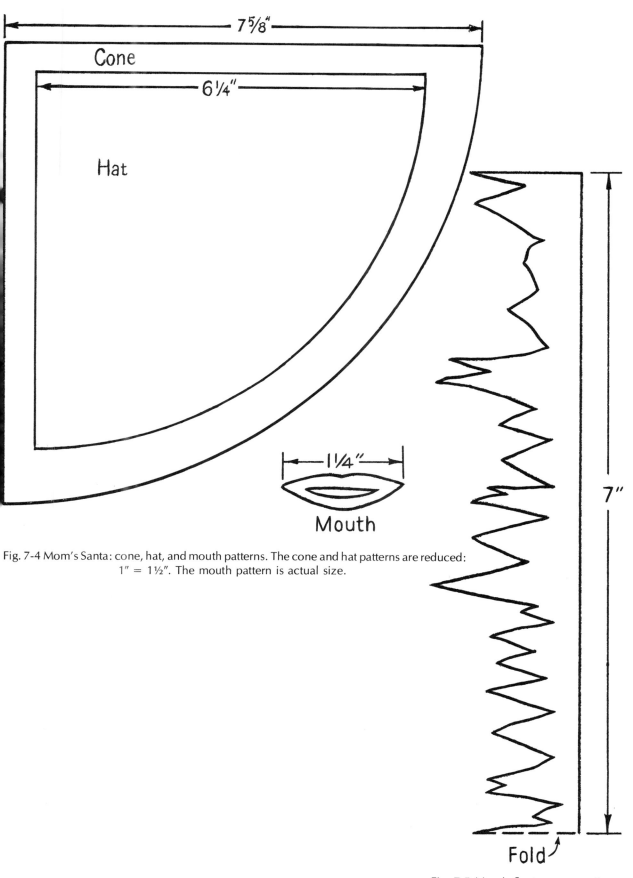

7⅝"

Cone

6¼"

Hat

1¼"

Mouth

7"

Fold

Fig. 7-4 Mom's Santa: cone, hat, and mouth patterns. The cone and hat patterns are reduced: 1″ = 1½″. The mouth pattern is actual size.

Fig. 7-5 Mom's Santa: snow pattern. This pattern is actual size.

Roll the poster board into a smooth cone shape. Overlap the seam ½ inch and secure with masking tape on both sides. Using the black felt tip pen, draw lines resembling a brick wall on the red felt cone. Lay the felt on the table with the brick work down. Apply glue to all outside edges of the felt. Roll the poster board over the felt, thus covering the cone. Secure the seam in the felt with glue.

Next, glue the felt snow at the cone opening with the straight edge at the top. Apply glue at random on the bricks and sprinkle diamond dust on it. Keeping the seam in back, punch one hole on each side just below the snow with the point of your scissors. Put the cord through the holes and knot each end. This is your hanger.

Glue the hatband on the curved edge of the hat. Roll the hat into a cone shape, securing the seam with glue. Attach the ball fringe to the peak of the hat using glue.

Apply glue around the inside rim of hat and position it on the Styrofoam ball.

Form the angel hair into a beard and attach it with glue. Then glue the mouth and eyes into place.

Now, glue the center of the red felt square over one end of the dowel. Tilt the head to one side and then glue it to the covered end of the dowel.

Place the dowel in the cone,
And you'll have a Santa of your own!

Large Pine Cone Tree

(SEE FRONT COVER)

This decoration has been very popular in nursing homes and with scout groups.

Materials

Large pine cone, approximately 4" × 7"	1 bunch yellow forget-me-nots
	1 dozen red berries
2 dozen small plastic green leaves	75" red yarn
1½ dozen white birthday candles	Silicone adhesive
1½ dozen large green sequins	

Cut birthday candles to ½ inch. Put a dab of silicone adhesive on the bottom of each candle and secure each one in the center of a large green sequin. Let dry. Cut the yarn into fifteen 5-inch pieces. Tie each piece into a bow.

Select a large pine cone that sets level on its stem end. Use silicone adhesive to attach all the trims to the cone. Put a candle at the very top of the pine cone and with a bow at each side of the base of the candle. Place the rest of the candles around the pine cone, about 1½ inches apart. Glue the yarn bows between the candles. Glue a small plastic green leaf with a red berry on top on the pine cone petals, alternating a leaf with a forget-me-not, all around the pine cone.

Allow the adhesive to dry completely before displaying the project.

Pearly Mouse
(SEE FRONT COVER)

Materials

Two 16mm pearls	2 plastic holly leaves with berries
2″ x 2″ white felt	Cotton ball
2″ x 2″ red felt	White glue
½″ x ½″ black felt	Toothpick

Put a dab of white glue on the top hole of one pearl and put the second pearl on top of the first, joining the pearls. Put a toothpick through holes in both pearls and hold tight. Spread glue on the bottom of one pearl and set it on a 2-inch circle, cut from red felt. Let this dry.

Cut a tail from the white felt, ⅛ by 2 inches. Also cut two small ears from the white felt. Now glue the tail and ears in position.

Cut a triangular shaped hat and a tiny dot from the red felt for a nose. Cut two tiny dots from the black felt for eyes. Glue eyes and the red nose on the top pearl.

Glue a small piece of cotton ball at the peak of the triangular hat. Then secure the hat in the center front of the ears. Glue holly leaves at the base of the mouse on the red felt circle.

Mousetrap

Materials

5″ x 11″ piece of old barn wood	2 miniature mice
1 yd of 3″ red print ribbon	4 kernels of corn
2″ x 5″ green foil paper	Wooden mousetrap
2″ x 3¼″ red construction paper	Metal picture hanger
1¾″ x 3″ white construction paper	Walnut stain
½″ x ½″ x 2″ Styrofoam block	Soft cloth
10″ of ⅛″ silver cord	Fine point pen
3″ of ¼″ red, green, and gold braid	Green ink
12″ of ¼″ red braid	White glue
4 stalks of wheat	

Fig. 7-6 Scoop, Christmas Birdhouse, Mousetrap, Kitchen Door.

Using a soft cloth, wipe the walnut stain into the barn wood and the wooden mousetrap. Allow the stain to dry. Attach the picture hanger on the back of the barn wood, near the top.

Cut a 12-inch length of the red print ribbon, cut an inverted V in one end of the ribbon. Spread glue on the back of the ribbon. Place the ribbon in the center of the barn wood lengthwise with the V notch at the bottom. Smooth out the ribbon and wrap the extra length over the top (Fig. 7-6).

Make a single loop bow with the remainder of the red print ribbon. Tie the center of the bow with 5 inches of the ¼-inch red braid. Now glue the bow on the center of the top edge of the barn wood plaque.

Glue the stained mousetrap in the center of the ribbon on the plaque. Slip the four pieces of wheat under the top right hand corner of the mousetrap. Place the heads of two wheat stalks toward the top left hand corner of the plaque and the heads of the other two stalks toward the lower right hand corner of the plaque. Press the mousetrap down firmly and hold for a minute.

123

Glue a miniature mouse 2 inches above the right hand corner of the mousetrap. Glue two kernels of corn in front of the mouse, leading to the trap. Make a small bow from a 3-inch length of ¼-inch red braid, and glue it at the neck of the mouse. This is Molly Mouse.

Glue the second mouse at the lower left hand corner of the trap. Glue two kernels of corn in front of the mouse, leading to the trap. Omit the bow on this mouse, because this is Billy Mouse.

Cut the Styrofoam into two one-inch long pieces. Wrap the Styrofoam pieces with green foil paper. Glue the loose edges down. Trim these packages with the silver cord. Glue one package on the trap at the lower right hand corner. Glue the other package on the plaque one inch above and to the left of the trap.

Following the pattern in Fig. 7-7, shape the red and white construction paper as a song book. Draw the music on the white paper, following the pattern with a fine point pen and green ink. Glue the white paper to the red and crease in the center. Glue the small red braid on the book as a bookmark. Glue the red, green, and gold braid onto the book at the crease. Now glue the song book onto the mousetrap on the upper left side.

Fig. 7-7 Mousetrap Song Book pattern. This pattern is actual size.

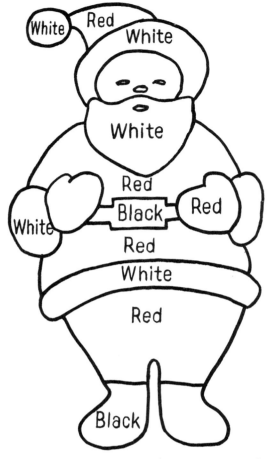

Fig. 7-8 Sandy Santa pattern. This pattern is actual size.

Sandy Santa

Working with sand is one of the newest crafts. Sand can be found in many colors at your local craft shop.

Materials

4″ × 6″ wooden plaque	Red, white, and black sand
Metal picture hanger	½″ paintbrush
Light green acrylic paint	¼″ paint brush
Dark green acrylic paint	#120 sandpaper
Flesh colored acrylic paint	White glue
Clear acrylic spray finish	

Nail the picture hanger on the back of the plaque. Sandpaper the plaque until it is very smooth; be sure to move the sandpaper with the grain of the wood. Wipe the wood clean with a damp cloth. Using the ½-inch brush, paint the front of the plaque with two coats of light green acrylic paint. Allow the first coat to dry for 30 minutes before applying the second coat. Paint the edges of the plaque with two coats of dark green. Allow the paint to dry.

Trace the pattern in Fig. 7-8 onto the plaque with carbon paper. Be very careful not to smear the plaque with the carbon paper.

Use the ¼-inch brush to paint the face area with the flesh colored acrylic paint. Let dry for 30 minutes. Clean the brush thoroughly.

Now place a large sheet of paper on your work area. Keep your plaque on the paper so that the excess sand is caught. You may then pour the sand back into its container for later use.

Use the ¼-inch brush to paint glue in all the areas marked red. Sprinkle red sand on the wet glue surface. Wait 5 minutes and then shake off the excess sand. Wait 20 minutes before applying the next color. To straighten any crooked edges, use a toothpick to brush off the excess sand. Repeat the above process for the black areas and then the white areas.

If you want to build up his tummy or the fur and mittens, put on more layers of glue and sand, letting layers dry between each application. Building up the Santa in these places adds another dimension.

When all is dry, spray the plaque with two light coats of clear acrylic paint. Try a design of your own, using the remaining sand.

Tinsel Tree Painting

Materials

6″ × 11″ unfinished wooden picture frame with glass	Red spray paint
	Gold spray paint
6″ × 11″ aluminum foil	Glass stain paints—yellow, light
Fine bristle brush	blue, dark green, red
Quill pen	Glass stain paint thinner
India ink, black waterproof	#120 sandpaper
White acrylic paint	Metal picture hanger

Remove the glass from the frame and set aside. Sand the frame with the #120 sandpaper until the surface is very smooth. Wipe the frame off with a clean, damp cloth. Spread newspapers over your work area and spray the frame with red paint (Fig. 4-5). Let the paint dry for 30 minutes. Now spray over the red very lightly with gold paint to give a speckled effect. Set aside and allow the paint to dry.

Clean the glass with a soft lint-free cloth and ammonia. Place the clean glass over the pattern. Be very careful not to get fingerprints on your clean glass. Trace the pattern in Fig. 7-9 onto the glass with the India ink. Let dry for 15 minutes.

126

Using the white acrylic paint, do the background, candles, roof of house, top of sleigh, and the flowers. Let these dry for 30 minutes. Paint second coat on the background. Let dry for 30 minutes.

With the glass stain paints color the following:

Bird, small balls—light blue
Top of tree, candle halos—yellow
House, sleigh, candy cane stripes, top and bottom of bucket,
   large balls—red
Tree—dark green

Clean the brush in the paint thinner between each color, wipe clean with a cloth. Do not paint the rope on the tree. Let dry overnight.

The aluminum foil should be the same size as the cardboard backing from the picture frame. Crumple the aluminum foil, then lay on table and smooth into a flat sheet. Wrap the foil around the cardboard and lay it against the painted side of the glass. Secure this into the frame tightly with the brads that came with the frame.

Put the picture hanger on the back and your picture is ready for hanging.

Designer Set

(SEE COLOR INSERT)

Materials

23" × 33" red felt	Cardboard roll from wax paper
5 yd of ½" silver braid	Clear acrylic spray
4 yd of 6 mm green sequins	Fabric protection spray
4 packages green, leaf-shaped sequins	Black felt pen
	White glue
9¾" diameter cardboard container or wastebasket	Toothpick

PLACE MAT

Cut a rectangle of red felt measuring 12 by 18 inches. Cut the 12-inch side along the 23-inch side of the big piece of felt so that the

Fig. 7-9 Tinsel Tree pattern. This pattern is actual size.

measurements will be right for the wastebasket. Cut a 60-inch length of silver braid. Spread glue around the edges of the red felt ½ inch from the sides. Then, lay the center of the silver braid into the glue. Let this dry.

Cut a 60-inch length of green sequins. With a toothpick, spread a thin line of glue along the center of the silver braid. Lay the green sequins on the glue. Let this dry.

Using the tree pattern from Millie's tree skirt (Fig. 6-4), draw the shape on the place mat in the lower left hand corner 3 inches from the bottom edge. Cut a piece of silver braid 18 inches long. Place a thin line of glue on the outline of the tree. Lay the silver braid on the glue.

To fill in your tree, use the leaf-shaped sequins. It should take seven or eight leaves to fill in the first row. With a toothpick, spread glue on one side of the sequins then lay the sequins on the felt inside the tree shape. Leave part of the silver braid exposed. Continue making rows of sequins until no red shows inside the shape.

For the tree trunk, cut a 1½-inch piece of silver braid. Round off two corners along one of the longer sides of the braid. Glue this below the tree with the rounded corners toward the bottom.

An alternate design can be made by using green felt with a red ball fringe border (see color insert). Place a small wreath of ball fringe in one corner of the place mat. Make a matching napkin ring and wastebasket using the same ball fringe motif.

NAPKIN RING

Cut a 2½-inch tube from the cardboard roll. Cut a piece of red felt measuring 2½ by 7 inches. Put white glue on the edges of the tube. Secure the red felt to the tube and glue the seam closed. Trim any excess felt.

Cut two lengths of silver braid each measuring 7 inches. Spread glue around the two edges of the red felt. Lay the silver braid into the glue. Cut two lengths of green sequins measuring 7 inches. Then, with a toothpick, spread a thin line of glue along the center of the silver braid. Lay the green sequins into the glue.

Using five leaf-shaped sequins, glue them into a tree shape opposite the seam in the felt.

WASTEBASKET

We used an empty potato chip container to complete our designer set. To seal the container so that it will make a handy holiday wastebasket, coat the inside with acrylic spray.

Cut a piece of red felt measuring 11 by 33 inches. Spread glue around both edges of the container. Lay the container on the felt with the bottom edge of the container matching one edge of the felt. Roll the container over the felt, pressing the edges firmly. Glue the seam closed. Fold the extra felt at the top to the inside of the container and glue in place.

Cut two lengths of silver braid 32 inches long. Also, cut two lengths of green sequins 32 inches long. Decorate the two edges of the container in the same manner described for the place mat.

On the opposite side of the container from the seam, draw a tree in the center like the one you drew on the place mat. Using an 18-inch piece of silver braid and about 55 leaf-shaped sequins, fill in the tree outline. Do not forget the tree trunk.

Spray all three pieces of your designer set with fabric spray to protect them from soiling.

Whitey Mouse

(SEE COLOR INSERT)

Materials

2" × 3" pink felt	Pink bead
2 sweet gum balls	White spray paint
Two 5mm wiggle eyes	Silicone adhesive

Spray paint the sweet gum balls white. Let dry. Use silicone adhesive to fasten gum balls together. Cut a ¼ by 3-inch piece from the pink felt. Use silicone adhesive and attach the felt to center end of a gum ball. This forms the tail.

Cut ears and two small circles from pink felt. Lay your index finger on the felt ear with tip of your finger toward straight edge of ear. Put a small amount of adhesive on straight edge. Place ears on gum ball in correct position. Hold for a minute. This shapes the ears.

Use adhesive to secure the small pink dots directly under the ears. Attach wiggle eyes to pink dots. Then glue the pink bead in position for the nose.

Be sure and make several—these will sell quickly at a bazaar.

White Squirrel

(SEE COLOR INSERT)

130

This is dedicated to my hometown, Olney, Illinois, where there are many white squirrels.

Materials

2 sweet gum balls
Small pine cone or acorn
Three 3" white single chenille
 bumps

6mm pink bead
Two 5mm wiggle eyes
Silicone adhesive
White spray paint

Spread newspapers on the floor and spray paint the sweet gum balls white. Let dry. Use silicone adhesive and glue the gum balls together.

Cut a ⅜-inch long piece from one end of two chenille bumps and dip one of the short pieces in adhesive. Push the sticky end into holes in top of a gum ball to form the ears. Put a small amount of adhesive on back of each wiggle eye and set into position. Do the same with the pink bead for the nose.

Shape the uncut chenille bump as a tail. Put adhesive on the very end and put under the bottom gum ball. Hold in place.

Put some adhesive on the uncut ends of the other two chenille bumps and lay one to each side of tail. Hold in place and then shape up over gum ball, gluing as you go. These are his paws. Turn down the loose ends and glue a small pine cone or an acorn in his paws.

Christmas Pin Cushion

(SEE COLOR INSERT)

Pin cushions make great gifts for that favorite teacher. This type is fun to make and will use up bits and pieces you may have left over from another project.

Materials

Two 2-piece Mason® or Ball®
 quart jar lids
5" × 10" green felt
20" single loop gold braid
1" diameter gold ring
4" × 8" of ½" thick foam rubber

1 dozen miniature gold pine
 cones
1 dozen holly berries
Masking tape
White glue

Cut two 3½-inch square pieces from the green felt and two 2½-inch round pieces from the foam rubber. Lay the felt and then the sponge rubber centered over the hole in the jar lid. Put the round flat piece of jar lid over sponge rubber. Press firmly into place, pushing in the center so as to make the felt go beyond the rim just a little. Repeat for the second jar lid. Fold excess felt to the inside. Put the two inside edges of the lid together and secure by pressing masking tape firmly over the entire seam where the two lids meet.

Cut a piece of green felt 1 by 10 inches. Glue this over the masking tape. Spread glue along edges of the green felt and lay single loops of gold braid into it. Remember to keep seams at the same place.

Cut wires from the miniature pine cones and holly berries. Put glue on each piece and arrange in a cluster over the seams. On the opposite side, glue the gold ring. This makes a stand for your pin cushion.

Creche Under Glass

(SEE COLOR INSERT)

Materials

4″ × 4″ red felt	Two plastic figures
Tinted roly-poly glass	Milkweed pod
4″ × 4″ × ½″ thick	6 holly berries
Styrofoam	Gold spray paint
11″ embroidered braid trim	White glue

To make a Styrofoam disk to fit the glass perfectly, press glass rim into the Styrofoam about ⅛ inch. Remove glass and using a serrated edge knife, completely cut out the disk.

Spray paint both sides of the Styrofoam disk and the milkweed pod gold. Allow to dry. Cut off part of the wide end of the milkweed pod so that the glass will fit over it. Spread glue on the cut end of the pod and attach it to the back center of the disk with outside of the pod to back of the disk. Hold until the glue starts to set. Now glue the figures in front of the milkweed pod. Glue three holly berries on the Styrofoam disk at the center front and the center back. Let all the glue dry before covering. If you cover with the glass too soon, the glass will become cloudy inside.

When all is dry, spread a small amount of glue on sides of the disk, invert the glass, and set it down over the decorated Styrofoam disk. Cut a 3-inch circle from the red felt and glue to bottom of the Styrofoam disk. Spread the glue on the embroidered braid and press firmly against the glass at the bottom, keeping the seam in the back.

Try this idea with any of the miniatures now available at craft shops.

Scoop

Look around in the barn or at a garage sale and maybe you'll find an old scoop with which to make an arrangement (Fig. 7-6). This is good for a table or to hang on a door.

Materials

26″ of 2″ green polka dot ribbon	3″ × 3″ Styrofoam block
26″ of 3″ red polka dot ribbon	Metal grain scoop
3 plastic pine picks	Adhesive floral clay
2 velvet apples on picks	6″ of #28 wire
3 velvet pears on picks	

Put two 2-inch strips of adhesive floral clay on the bottom of the Styrofoam block and press the block in center of the scoop. Make sure it adheres tightly.

Push one plastic pine pick into each side of the Styrofoam at the front. Put the other pine pick at the center top. Push the three green pears into Styrofoam at the center front, between the two pine picks. Then place the apples into the Styrofoam on each side.

Center the green polka dot ribbon on the top of the red polka dot ribbon. Make a single loop bow. Tie the bow in the middle by twisting wire around the ribbon. Place the bow at the top center with some greens coming from behind the bow. Use the extra wire to fasten the bow by pushing the wire into the Styrofoam.

Christmas Song Book

Materials

6″ × 10″ Styrofoam opened book shape	25 small green sequins
7″ × 20″ white felt	56 small gold sequins
20″ of 1½″ gold ribbon	10 large gold sequins
14″ of ½″ flat gold braid	5 red spoke sequins
12″ red tinsel wire	Straight pins
2⅓ yd green plastic bead cord	White glue
1 package green rocaille beads	1″ paint brush

Cut the 1½-inch gold ribbon into two 10-inch lengths. Brush glue onto the top and bottom edges of the book. Lay one piece of the ribbon onto the glue on each edge, smooth out, and allow to dry. Trim off excess ribbon to match the shape of the opened book edge (Fig. 4-1).

Cut the white felt into two 7 by 10-inch pieces. Brush glue on the back side of the book, lay one piece of felt onto the glue, press down, and smooth out wrinkles. Trim off excess felt at edges and set aside to dry.

You will need a ruler and a pencil with a sharp point to layout and mark the music staff lines on the other piece of felt. Lay the felt lengthwise in front of you. Draw the first staff line 8 inches long, 1½ inches down from the top of the felt. This line is centered on the felt with the ends one inch from each edge of the felt. Now draw the remaining four staff lines with a ⅜-inch space between each line.

Next measure down 1¼ inches from the last staff line and draw five more staff lines with ⅜-inch space between each line.

Brush glue over the front side of the book. Lay the marked piece of felt onto the glue very carefully.

Be sure that the top of the felt and the top edge of the book are even. Also, check your staff lines to be sure they are lined up straight across the book. Smooth out the wrinkles. The side edges should also be even. Allow to dry and trim off any excess felt.

Cut the gold braid into two 7-inch lengths. Place glue on one side of the braid and fasten to the side edges of the book, overlapping the felt on the front and back. Smooth out and press firmly.

Cut ten 8-inch lengths of green plastic bead cord. Glue one piece of cord onto each of the penciled lines. To complete the staff lines, place a rocaille bead and then a small green sequin onto a straight pin. Now push the pin into the Styrofoam at the end of a staff line. Repeat until a bead, sequin, and pin has been placed at the end of every line.

Glue three red spoke sequins at the top center of the book and two at the bottom center. Place a rocaille bead and a green sequin on a straight pin. Push the pin through the center of the spoke sequin.

Cut the red tinsel wire into two 6-inch lengths. Shape a treble clef from each length of wire and glue near the left end of each staff. You may wish to pin the wire down until the glue is dry.

Choose the song you wish to use from any Christmas songbook. I chose Jingle Bells. Using a pencil, lightly write the name of the song across the top of the felt. Try to space the song title evenly. Place a rocaille bead onto a straight pin and push the pin into the Styrofoam, setting beads and pins close to each other along the pencil outline to complete the song title.

The musical notes are formed by using straight pins with the large and small gold sequins. Lightly pencil in the musical notes. Fasten the large gold sequins in position to form the head of the musical note. Using the small gold sequins, fasten them to form the stem and flag of the notes.

You may wish to spray your completed project with a fabric protector to help keep your new decoration clean.

Corn Mouse

(SEE FRONT COVER)

Materials

½" × ½" red felt	2 blue sequins
3" plastic corn	4 red holly berries
3" red chenille bump	Silicone adhesive

If there is a wire on the plastic corn, discard it. Lay corn on its side. Put some adhesive on the small end of four red holly berries. Attach to the corn in position for feet. Glue the red chenille bump at the large end of the corn for the tail. Let adhesive dry and then curl chenille bump into a tail.

Cut two small ears from the red felt. Just a dab of adhesive will hold the ears upright at small end of the corn. Then glue the blue sequins in place for eyes and a tiny piece of red felt for a nose.

This really is a quicky bazaar idea.

Door Knob Decorations

Chapter 8

Little Girl's Decoration

(SEE BACK COVER)

Materials

10″ × 12″ red felt	Blue sequin
Flesh colored felt	Red bell
28″ gold rickrack	Cotton dress material
4″ red and gold rickrack	3 cotton balls
16″ brown yarn	White glue

This door knob decoration will delight any little girl. You may make it any colors to match her room.

Cut the door knob decoration base from the red felt (Fig. 8-1). Spread glue at the edges of the cut out piece and lay it on the remaining piece of red felt. When the glue has dried, trim the second piece of felt to match.

Fold the round part of the decoration in half and cut a one-inch long slit at the center through all thicknesses. Now fold the round part

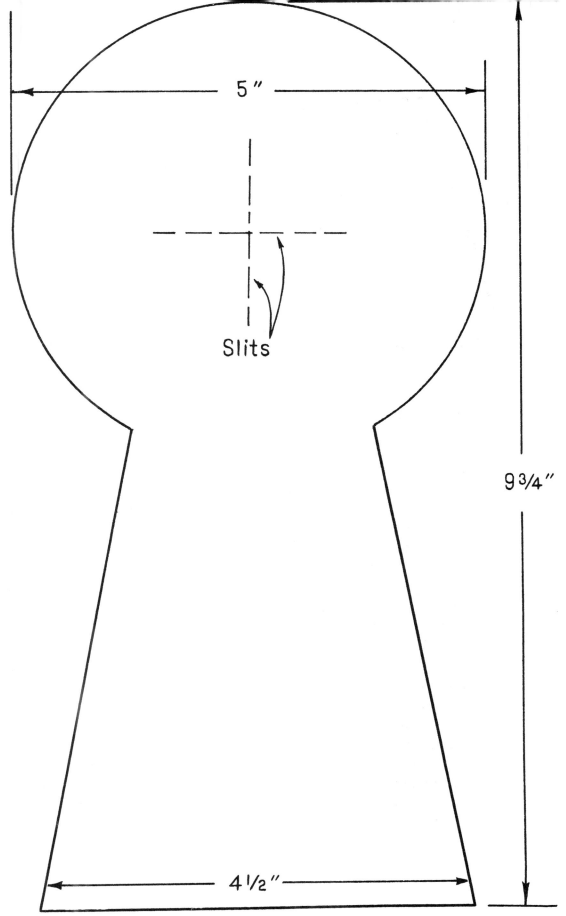

5″

Slits

9¾″

4½″

Fig. 8-1 Door Knob Decoration base pattern. This pattern is actual size.

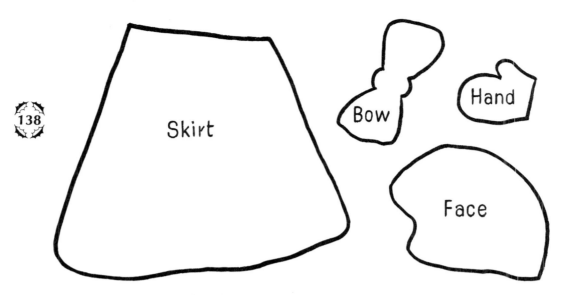

Fig. 8-2 Little Girl's Decoration patterns. These patterns are actual size.

in the opposite direction and cut a second one-inch long slit. This forms the cross-cut opening through which the door knob will slip.

Glue the gold rickrack at the edge all around the decoration base. Cut face and hands from flesh colored felt (Fig. 8-2). Cut bow and skirt from the cotton dress material. Glue red and gold rickrack along bottom edge of skirt. Spread glue on the three edges of the skirt on the back of the material, leaving the bottom edge open. Place the skirt on the red felt, ½ inch in from each side and ½ inch up from the bottom. The skirt will not lay flat. Press the edges down firmly. Squirt some glue underneath the skirt and push the three cotton balls in under the skirt. This will pad the skirt to make it stand out. Be sure that none of the cotton shows below the bottom of the skirt.

Glue the hand in position on the skirt. Remember to keep the thumb to the top. Glue face in proper position, keeping nose in the right place.

Play with the yarn before you glue it in place—decide just what kind of hair style you want. I cut the yarn in four lengths and glued it in place for a simple hairdo with bangs and long flowing hair.

Now you are ready to glue the hair bow in place, then center the bell on the bow, and attach with glue. Use a toothpick to put a dab of glue on the blue sequin and then place on the face for her eye. Isn't she cute?

Fishin' Boy

(SEE BACK COVER)

Materials

10″ × 12″ white felt
1″ × 2″ brown felt
2″ × 2″ flesh felt
2″ × 3″ royal blue felt
2″ × 3″ light blue felt
1⅓ yd of ¼″ wide light blue
    rickrack with adhesive back

1 yd of ⅛″ wide royal blue flat
    braid
8″ gold tinsel braid
2 gold bells
White glue
Toothpick

139

Cut out one door knob decoration base from the white felt, following the pattern outline in Fig. 8-1. Place white glue around the edge of the cut out piece and then lay this piece on to the remaining piece of white felt. Allow to dry. Cut the second piece, closely following the pattern outline of the first piece. Cut slits in the round top so that the decoration may slip over a door knob.

Start trimming the decoration by placing the rickrack around the edge of the white felt. Pull one inch of adhesive back from the light blue rickrack. Starting at a corner, press the rickrack onto the edge of the white felt. Continue pulling adhesive back and pressing rickrack firmly all around the edge.

Next, glue the royal blue flat braid just to the inside of the rickrack. The remaining light blue rickrack is placed between the cross cut slits to form an X.

Cut the following parts, using the pattern outline in Fig. 8-3.

Hat, brown felt
Face, hands, and feet, flesh felt

Shirt, royal blue felt
Trousers, light blue felt

Following the pattern as a guide, position all parts of the boy onto the white felt. Glue the feet onto the white felt base first, ½ inch from the left side and extending ⅛ inch over the bottom royal blue braid. Next, glue the trousers, overlapping the top of the feet ⅛ inch. Using a felt tip pen, mark the trouser leg line. Glue the jacket overlapping the top of the trousers. Do not glue the jacket neckline and sleeve cuff at this time.

Now glue the face in position and glue the hat over the boy's head. Next glue jacket neckline.

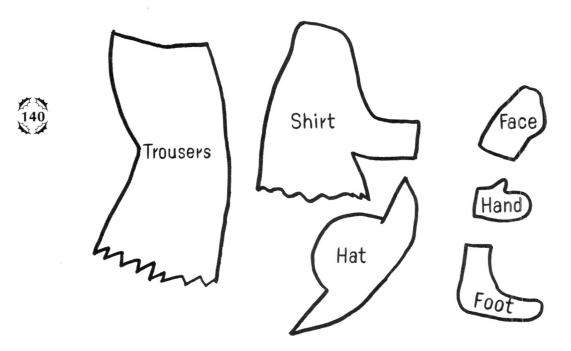

Fig. 8-3 Fishin' Boy patterns. These patterns are actual size.

Paint the toothpick black with a felt tip pen. Glue boy's hand in place. While glue is still wet, slip large end of toothpick underneath hand. Place a small amount of glue onto other end of toothpick and place on boy's shoulder. Now glue the jacket cuff into place.

Put a small amount of glue on all but 2 inches of the gold tinsel braid. Attach one end of the braid to the fishing pole. Curve the rest of the braid down behind the boy and fasten to the white felt. Allow the glue to dry. Tie the two gold bells at the end of the braid.

Now your door knob decoration is ready to be hung on the door to your favorite little boy's room.

Door Knob Wreath

(SEE BACK COVER)

Materials

24" of 6" wide green, water repellent, velvet-type ribbon
1⅔ yd of ½" red velvet ribbon

9 small artificial fruit
6" #28 wire
6" × 6" poster board
White glue

Cut a 5-inch diameter circle from the poster board. Next cut a 1½-inch diameter hole from the center of the 5-inch circle. Using this 5-inch ring as a pattern, cut two pieces from the green velvet ribbon. Glue one piece of ribbon onto each side of the poster board. Allow to dry. Cut a slit from the outside edge to the center. This will allow you to slip the decoration over your door knob.

Cut thirty petals, using the pattern in Fig. 8-4, from the remaining green velvet ribbon. Place glue on the straight edge of the petals. Starting at the slit, place a row of petals around the outside edge of the ring. Glue the petals so that one inch of the pointed end of each petal extends beyond the outside edge and so that each petal overlaps the one adjacent by ⅛ inch.

Now glue a second row of petals onto the ring. Place this row with the straight edge of the petal even with the inner edge of the ring. Glue the petals all the way around the ring, with each petal overlapping the adjacent one by ⅛ inch.

Make a triple loop bow from the red velvet ribbon, leaving 12-inch streamers. Wrap the #28 wire around the center of the bow and twist tightly. Glue the bow just to the left of the slit in the ring. The bow marks the bottom center of the ring. Glue three pieces of artificial fruit at the top center of the ring and three at each side center also. Allow the glue to dry.

This is an excellent trim for the kitchen door.

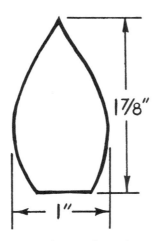

Fig. 8-4 Door Knob Wreath petal pattern.
This pattern is actual size.

Christmas Tree Door Knob Trim

(SEE BACK COVER)

Materials

5″ × 12″ white fake fur	4 red spoke sequins
3″ × 5″ green felt	3 gold spoke sequins
1 yd gold eyelash braid	Eleven 4mm pearls
1½ red tinsel braid	White glue
½ yd gold tinsel braid	

Following the pattern in Fig. 8-5, cut one door knob trim base from the white fake fur. As previously described, form the cross-cut opening so it can be slipped over the door knob.

Glue the gold eyelash braid on the back of the fake fur. Glue only the flat part, keeping the loops extended beyond the outside edge of the fake fur. Glue the red tinsel braid on the front at the edge. Also, glue a length of red tinsel braid in a circle around the cross out slits in the top. Set aside to dry.

Cut a tree outline from the green felt, using tree pattern in Fig. 6-4. Glue the tree in center of the lower section of the door knob trim. Glue gold tinsel braid around the edge of the green felt.

Glue one gold spoke sequin at the top of the green felt for a star. One inch directly below the gold sequin, glue one red spoke sequin. Glue three red sequins in a row ½ inch above the bottom of the green felt. Next glue two gold sequins in a row one inch above the bottom row of the red sequins. Now glue one 4 mm pearl in the center of each sequin. Finally glue four pearls vertically in the center of the tree trunk section.

Angel Door Knob Decoration

(SEE BACK COVER)

Materials

10″ × 12″ lavender felt	1 package hot pink sequins
1 yd gold double loop braid	1 package turquoise sequins
5″ tall gold plastic angel	White glue
1 red sequin	

Cut out the door knob base from the lavender felt, following the pattern outline in Fig. 8-1. Place glue around the edge of this piece of

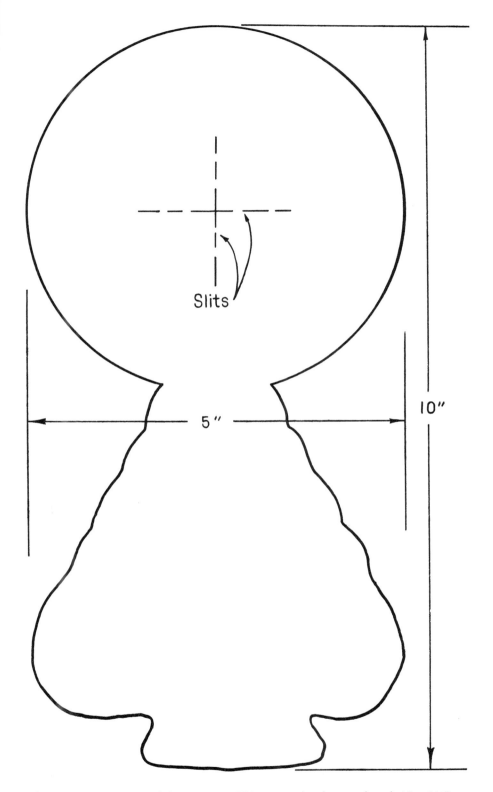

Fig. 8-5 Christmas Tree Door Knob base pattern. This pattern has been reduced: 1″ = 1¼″

felt. Lay this piece onto the remaining felt and allow glue to dry. Now cut the second piece of felt, following the outline of the first piece very closely. Cut cross slits in the round top part of the base to slip the decoration over a door knob.

Spread glue around the edge of the base and lay the gold braid onto the glue. Press the braid firmly and allow the glue to dry.

Lay the angel onto the bottom part of the base. Position the angel in the center and ½ inch from the bottom of the base. Mark the position of the angel lightly with a pencil. Remove the angel and spread glue over the back of the figure. Place in position on the felt base and press down firmly.

Cut a pie-shaped wedge from the red sequin and discard the wedge shape. The remaining piece is the angel's mouth. Glue it in place.

Glue turquoise sequins around the angel's head for a halo. Also, glue turquoise sequins on the angel's skirt, following the skirt designs. Glue the hot pink sequins on the hem of both the sleeves and skirt.

Your angel is now ready for display at an entranceway or bedroom door.

Born and raised in Olney, Illinois, Jane Berry began making handcrafts as a young girl. Since her marriage in 1951, Jane has been busy raising five children, decorating their home with handcrafted items, and outfitting the family with home sewn fashions.

After her children were all enrolled in school, Jane held her first job in a craft shop in Livonia, Michigan. After relocating to the Media, Pennsylvania, area, she worked for various retail craft outlets and began teaching craft skills and demonstrating new products and methods.

Teaching has brought Jane into contact with scout groups, women's clubs, and evening adult classes. She has contributed short articles to *Creative Crafts Magazine* and is presently a designer for D. Jay Products, Inc.

Jane's varied audiences include educational television viewers; cruise ship classes; and numerous exhibits, bazaars, and trade fairs.